Books by Eric Hammel

76 Hours: The Invasion of Tarawa (with John E. Lane)

Chosin: Heroic Ordeal of the Korean War

The Root: The Marines in Beirut

Ace!: A Marine Night-Fighter Pilot in World War II

(with R. Bruce Porter)

Duel for the Golan (with Jerry Asher)

Guadalcanal: Starvation Island

Guadalcanal: The Carrier Battles

Guadalcanal: Decision at Sea

Munda Trail: The New Georgia Campaign

The Jolly Rogers (with Tom Blackburn)

Khe Sanh: Siege in the Clouds

First Across the Rhine (with David E. Pergrin)

Lima-6: A Marine Company Commander in Vietnam

(with Richard D. Camp)

Ambush Valley

Aces Against Japan

Aces Against Japan II

Aces Against Germany

Air War Europa: Chronology

Carrier Clash

Aces at War

Air War Pacific: Chronology

Aces in Combat

Bloody Tarawa (with John E. Lane)

Marines at War

Carrier Strike

Pacific Warriors: The U.S. Marines in World War II

Iwo Jima: Portrait of a Battle

Marines in Hue City: A Portrait of Urban Combat, Tet 1968

Guadalcanal: The U.S. Marines in World War II

New Georgia, Bougainville, and Cape Gloucester: The U.S. Marines in World War II

THE U.S. MARINES IN WORLD WAR II

TARAWA AND THE MARSHALLS

A PICTORIAL TRIBUTE

ERIC HAMMEL

CRESTLINE

*This book is respectfully dedicated to the gallant American soldiers, sailors, airmen,
and Marines who achieved victory in the Pacific.*

This edition published in 2013 by CRESTLINE
a division of BOOK SALES, Inc.
276 Fifth Avenue Suite 206
New York, New York 10001
USA

This edition published by arrangement with Zenith Press, an imprint of MBI Publishing Company

First published in 2008 by Zenith Press, an imprint of MBI Publishing Company,
400 First Avenue North, Suite 400, Minneapolis, MN 55401 USA

Copyright © 2008 by Eric Hammel

Library of Congress Cataloging-in-Publication Data

Hammel, Eric M.
 Tarawa and the Marshalls : a pictorial tribute / Eric Hammel.
   p. cm.
 Includes bibliographical references and index.
 ISBN 978-0-7858-3073-3
1. United States. Marine Corps—History—World War, 1939–1945. 2. United States. Marine
Corps—History—World War, 1939–1945—Pictorial works. 3. Tarawa, Battle of, Kiribati, 1943.
4. Tarawa, Battle of, Kiribati, 1943—Pictorial works. 5. World War, 1939-1945—Campaigns—
Marshall Islands. 6. World War, 1939–1945—Campaigns--Marshall Islands—Pictorial works. I.
Title. II. Title: U.S. Marines in World War II. III. Title: United States Marines in World War II.
D769.369.H36 2008
 940.54'26681—dc22
          2008015726

Maps by: Phil Schwartzberg, Meridian Maps

On the cover, frontispiece, title page, and back cover: *Official USMC Photos*

Editor: Scott Pearson
Designer: Jennie Tischler

Printed in China

Contents

Author's Note

This is the beginning of the war the Marine Corps intended to fight and to which it devoted decades of planning and doctrinal development: an island-hopping drive across the central Pacific. The plan specifically targeted the Japanese mandate in the Marshall Islands as a steppingstone to the Marianas, then onward toward Japan. The idea was to outflank the Caroline Islands from the north and, especially, cut the naval and air routes between Japan and its naval bastion at Truk.

As events unfolded, the Allies were long delayed in even setting the conditions for the planned advance through the central Pacific. Events well to the south required a response in the Solomon Islands and New Guinea, and that required two years of bloody warfare with every soldier, sailor, Marine, ship, and airplane the United States could dispatch to that distant region's far-flung battlefields.

When it came time to devote assets to the central Pacific, once a command and planning structure was in place, the first order of business turned out to be the Gilbert Islands, a patchwork of British-mandated atolls the Imperial Navy had swiftly conquered at the outset of the Pacific War. The Gilberts were well to the east of the Marshalls, but they were within range of modern aircraft, which made them a useful if time-consuming preliminary target.

During the first fourteen months of the Pacific War, which ended in an American victory at Guadalcanal, the Marine Corps devoted few resources to documenting the war on film. Very few photographers were deployed to the Pacific, and they were neither trained nor often called upon to act as *combat* photographers. That worldview, the name, and the training to go with it, did not really emerge in the field until late 1943, at Bougainville and Tarawa. The former has been covered in the second volume of this series, and Tarawa has been covered in great detail in *Bloody Tarawa*, which I wrote years ago with the late John E. Lane, a Tarawa combat veteran.

To satisfy the needs of the current series, as well as to provide a capsule view of the Tarawa ordeal for readers unfamiliar with the story, half of this volume is devoted to the seventy-six-hour battle. I have attempted to locate photos that do not appear in *Bloody Tarawa*, and I have indeed located several dozen. Perhaps these will find favor among the many, many readers of that book, which is one of my personal favorites from among my own works.

The photographic record that started so slowly and unevenly at Guadalcanal and on through the central Solomons perked up in late 1943, at Bougainville and Tarawa, as more and better-organized photographers with a better idea about what to photograph moved into battle with Marine combat units. The photographic record is much larger and actually mounts in intensity as one follows the Marines across the wide Pacific. The photos are of better quality, more immediate, more sympathetic toward the combat Marines who have to assault the beaches, brave the fire, take the hills, comb the valleys and forests, and reduce all manner of Japanese defensive schemes that mark the long, long road to victory. They become more knowing and more insightful as the photographers begin to share the day-to-day, moment-by-moment life-and-death struggles their combatant comrades are thrown into. That will be evident as you encounter the photographic record in this volume.

Eric Hammel
Northern California
Fall 2007

Acknowledgments

For priceless help in accessing and scanning photos in official collections, I thank Theresa M. Roy and Holly Reed at the Still Pictures branch of the National Archives and Records Administration; Mike Miller, Patricia Mullen, and Sue Dillon at the Marine Corps University Archive at Quantico, Virginia; Colonel Walt Ford and Nancy Hoffman at *Leatherneck Magazine;* and Colonel Dick Camp and Lena Kaljot at the Marine Corps Historical Division.

Glossary and Guide to Abbreviations

VMAC	V Marine Amphibious Corps
A6M	Imperial Navy Mitsubishi "Zero" fighter
Amtrac	Amphibian tractor
Avenger	U.S. Navy/Marine Grumman TBF carrier torpedo/light bomber
B-24	U.S. Army Air Forces Consolidated Liberator four-engine heavy bomber
BAR	U.S. .30-caliber Browning automatic rifle
Betty	Imperial Navy Mitsubishi G4M twin-engine land attack bomber
Catalina	U.S. Navy Consolidated PBY twin-engine amphibious patrol bomber
D-day	Invasion day
D+1, etc.	The day after D-day, etc.
D3A	Imperial Navy Aichi Val dive-bomber
Dauntless	U.S. Navy/Marine Douglas SBD dive-bomber
F4U	U.S. Navy/Marine Vought Corsair fighter
F6F	U.S. Navy Grumman Hellcat fighter
G4M	Imperial Navy Mitsubishi Betty twin-engine land attack bomber
Hellcat	U.S. Navy Grumman F6F fighter
LCI(G)	Landing craft, infantry (gunboat) armed with 20mm and 40mm cannon
LCI(R)	Landing craft, infantry (rocket) armed with 4.5-inch rockets
LCM	Landing craft, medium
LCT	Landing craft, tank
LCVP	Landing craft, vehicle, personnel
LST	Landing ship, tank
LVT	Landing vehicle, tracked; amphibian tractor; amtrac
LVT(A)	Armored amphibian tractor (i.e., amphibian tank)
M1	U.S. Garand .30-caliber semiautomatic rifle
M3	U.S. Stuart light tank
M3	U.S. 75mm tank destroyer halftrack
M4	U.S. Sherman medium tank
Mitchell	U.S. Army Air Forces North American B-25 twin-engine medium bomber
PBY	U.S. Navy Consolidated Catalina twin-engine amphibious patrol bomber
Pioneers	U.S. Marine shore party troops
R4D	U.S. Navy/Marine Douglas Dakota twin-engine transport
SBD	U.S. Navy/Marine Douglas Dauntless dive-bomber
Seabees	Members of U.S. Navy construction battalions (CBs)
TBF	U.S. Navy/Marine Grumman Avenger carrier torpedo/light bomber
UDT	U.S. Navy underwater demolition team
Val	Imperial Navy Aichi D3A carrier dive-bomber
VF	U.S. Navy fighting squadron
Zero	Imperial Navy Mitsubishi A6M fighter

Maps

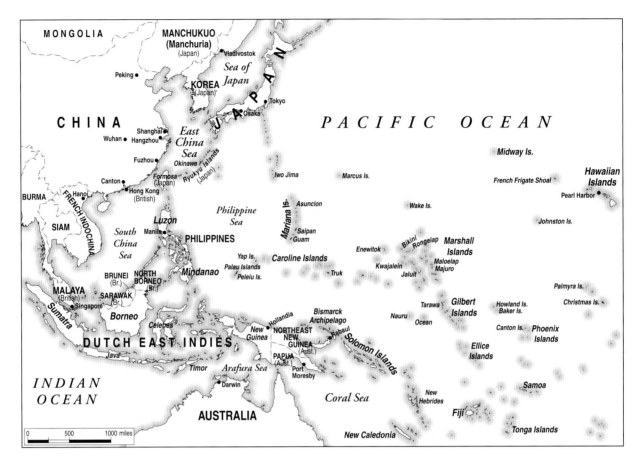

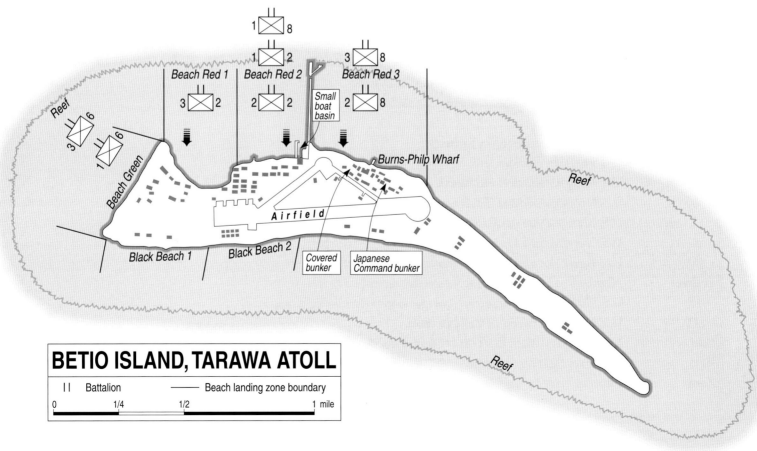

BETIO ISLAND, TARAWA ATOLL

II Battalion	—— Beach landing zone boundary

0   1/4   1/2   1 mile

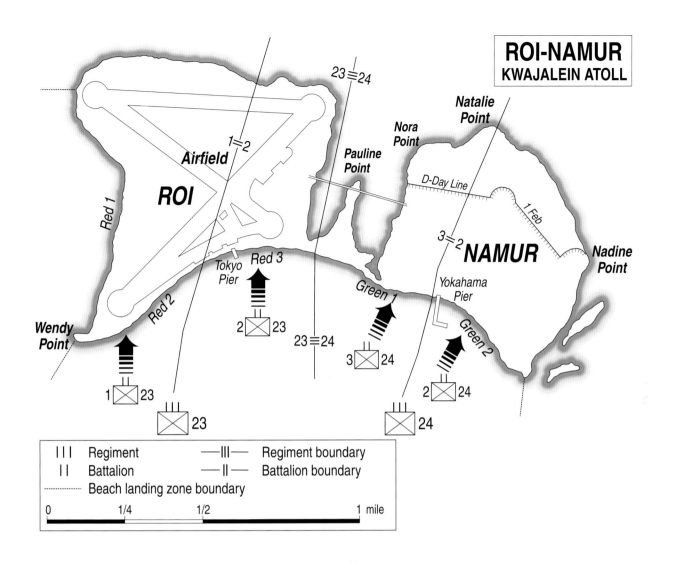

ROI

Airfield

Red 1

Red 2

Red 3

Wendy Point

Tokyo Pier

1⬛2

Pauline Point

Nora Point

Natalie Point

D-Day Line

1 Feb

NAMUR

3⬛2

Nadine Point

Yokahama Pier

Green 1

Green 2

23⬛24

1⬛23

⬛ 23

2⬛23

3⬛24

2⬛24

⬛ 24

⦀	Regiment	—Ⅲ—	Regiment boundary
ⅠⅠ	Battalion	—ⅠⅠ—	Battalion boundary
----	Beach landing zone boundary		

0   1/4   1/2   1 mile

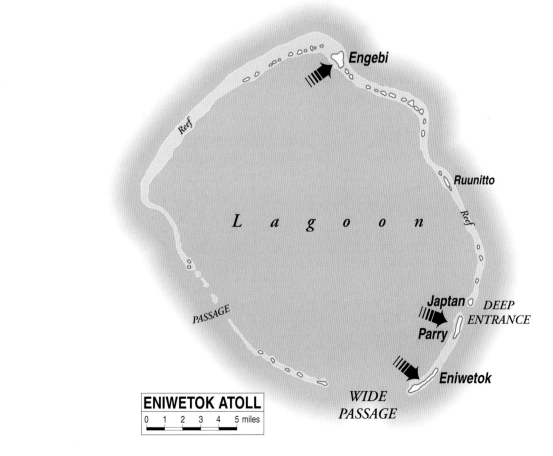

Engebi

Reef

Ruunitto

Reef

L a g o o n

PASSAGE

Japtan

DEEP ENTRANCE

Parry

Eniwetok

WIDE PASSAGE

ENIWETOK ATOLL

0 1 2 3 4 5 miles

CHAPTER 1

Tarawa

BEFORE

Following the bloodless seizure of the Ellice Islands in October 1942, the first offensive in the long-planned, long-delayed push across the central Pacific was in the former British mandate in the Gilbert Islands—simultaneous landings in Makin Atoll by elements of the U.S. Army's 27th Infantry Division and at Tarawa Atoll by the 2d Marine Division. The Gilbert Islands, positioned at the eastern edge of Japanese-held territory in the central Pacific, were selected as targets because the invasion could be supported by long-range bombers operating from the Ellice Islands and would, in its turn, support long-range bombing missions against Japanese-held atolls in the eastern Marshall Islands.

Betio Island, as seen from an Army Air Forces B-24 during a bombing mission in September 1943. The view is roughly west to east, with the landing beaches on the left (north) and the airfield clearly delineated. *Official Signal Corps Photo*

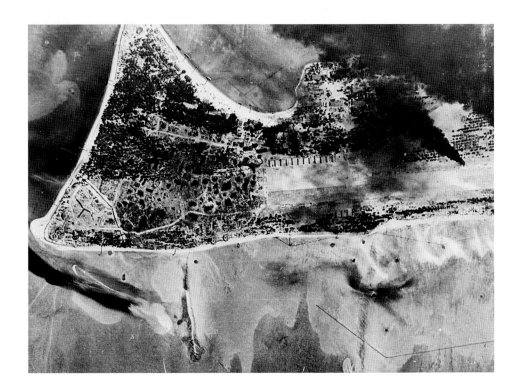

The western half of Betio (i.e., the invasion area) as seen from a B-24 during a bombing mission in October 1943. The invasion beaches are at the top of the photo (north) and run from left (west) to right: Red-1, Red-2, and Red-3 (obscured by smoke). Some barbed-wire barriers, trenches, and roadways can be seen. The T-shaped structures along the beaches are overwater latrines. *Official Signal Corps Photo*

Betio's first line of defense, literally, was the seawall that surrounded the island. This stretch of seawall on Beach Red-1 shows a typical layout: sand-reinforced log pillbox to the right and evenly spaced embrasures for small troop positions running along the entire section of the wall. Note the barbed wire set to ensnare invaders during the landing. Most defensive emplacements on Betio were built from the thousands of coconut palms that had to be removed to make room for the airfield, administration buildings, and bivouac areas. *Official USMC Photo*

The Gilberts invasion, which opened on November 20, 1943, was the Marine Corps' first "classic" amphibious assault over a reef against a defended beach. As such, it represented the pinnacle of achievement to that time in the practice of amphibious warfare. The invasion of Tarawa was as much a test of the doctrine, training, and equipment of the Marine Corps as it was an example of the bold seizure of a heavily defended island air base.

The U.S. Navy assembled the largest bombardment force seen in the Pacific to that time: several battleships mounting 14- or 16-inch guns, cruisers with 6- and 8-inch batteries, and destroyers with 5-inch batteries for close-in work. A flotilla of aircraft carriers, each brimming with light bombers and fighters, would be on hand to soften the way and provide close air support, which was an emerging doctrine that was itself to be tested fully at Tarawa. So powerful did the bombardment force appear that

A closer look at a firing embrasure on a small troop position built into the seawall. The aperture is about eight inches high. *Official USMC Photo*

This is a troop bunker or ammunition storage with a short trench and open firing position constructed of sandbags, corrugated iron, coconut logs, and milled wood. *Official USMC Photo*

very senior navy officers boasted that the Marines would be needed only to go ashore to pick up the pieces.

In the two days before the reinforced 2d Marine Division was to land, the battleships, cruisers, destroyers, fighters, and bombers undertook the most massive bombardment any navy had ever hurled at any shore target. The tiny island of Betio, little more than 2 acres in size, was, it was assumed, pulverized. The five thousand–man Japanese garrison (three thousand Imperial Navy infantrymen and two thousand construction and base troops) was thought to be destroyed.

continued on page 28

This is the firing embrasure for a log pillbox set up to accommodate a heavy machine gun. *Official USMC Photo*

This above-ground troop shelter features a splinter wall and protected entry. Betio's water table was quite high, so most bunkers had to be built atop the ground. Many, however, were covered with deep layers of sand for both blast protection and camouflage. *Official USMC Photo*

Above: This concrete pillbox, built to accommodate a light machine gun with crew, was probably prefabricated in Japan. The rear exit leads into a coconut-log bunker built into the seawall. Coral blocks and rough stones were often used as fill between double log containment walls. *Official USMC Photo*

This prefabricated steel pillbox is one of a half dozen that were spotted around the island to serve as local command posts. *Official USMC Photo*

This rare captured photo shows gunners test-firing a large-caliber naval gun. Note how neat the surroundings are—a tropical paradise. *Marine Corps University Archive*

Below: This 80mm antiboat gun is one of many beachside heavy weapons set in to fire at large vessels and landing craft. Fortunately for Marines, most were deployed without overhead cover or decent camouflage, so they were early victims of prelanding bombardment. *Official USMC Photo*

The Tarawa invasion armada as seen at dawn over the breech of a 20mm antiaircraft cannon aboard one of the troop transports. *Official USMC Photo*

Opposite: The 2d Amphibious Tractor Battalion deployed seventy-five LVT-1 amtracs aboard the transports sailing from Wellington. These vehicles, armored with boilerplate, supported four machine guns—two .50-caliber weapons on the forward bulkhead of the troop compartment and one on each side bulkhead. Joining the LVT-1s along the way were fifty more powerful and factory-armored LVT-2s rushed from the United States to make their combat debut at Tarawa. The LVT-1 had been designed and produced as an amphibian truck, not as an assault vehicle. But use of amtracs in ad hoc assault roles in the Solomon Islands had led to a reassessment of their true potential. Their first intentional use in a combat assault was at Tarawa. *Official USMC Photo*

Clean-cut teenage American boys having the time of their lives—so far. *Official USMC Photo*

Landing craft crews are briefed on their D-day tasks. *Official USMC Photo*

Carrier aircraft bore a large burden during the two-day prelanding bombardment that was supposed to turn Betio into a sterile lump of coral and sand. One F6F Hellcat fighter pilot said later that the island looked like a tropical paradise when he saw it the first time and a full ashtray when he left. *Official U.S. Navy Photo*

A 5-inch mount aboard battleship *Maryland* works out against Betio. The fact that the low-slung target is within eyeball range of the gunners clearly shows the ascendance of bravado over gunnery. Flat-trajectory rounds of all sizes tended to carom across the low, featureless spit of sand rather than detonate on the defenses. *Official USMC Photo*

A photographer aboard a light spotting plane off southern Betio captures a prelanding phase of the bombardment as the fleet makes ready to land the landing force. The white smoke across the center of the view is from a fire in a building beside the boat basin at the foot of Betio's five-hundred-yard-long pier. Beach Red-3 is to the right (east) of the pier, Red-2 is to the left, and Red-1 begins well to the left of the photo. *Official U.S. Navy Photo*

Smoke from numerous fires obscures much of the northern beaches, but a large portion of the main runway and a line of aircraft revetments can be seen. Above the rightmost revetments, near the center of the photo, is the boundary of Beaches Red-1 (left) and Red-2. *Official U.S. Navy Photo*

Below: Huge pillars of smoke from at least four large fires envelop the western end of Betio. The point of land in the center of the photo marks Betio's southwestern corner. Beach Green is to the left, and the unused Beach Black-1 curves away to the right. *Official U.S. Navy Photo*

This photo was taken on D+3 toward Betio's tapering eastern end. It looks more or less like the entire island was supposed to look like before H-hour on D-day. It looks this way because the navy gunners' bravado ceased the moment Marines wearing only their shirts for armor encountered fire from the hundreds of emplacements that had *not* been hit during the prelanding bombardment. So with the blood-soaked lesson firmly in mind, the naval gunners and carrier airmen worked over the eastern end of the island without the bravado, just with cold, calculated efficiency. And this was the result—a moonscape of large shell craters from 14-inch and 16-inch rounds mixed in with damage from smaller naval rounds and bombs and rockets delivered by air. *Official U.S. Navy Photo*

For all that naval gunfire failed the Marines, there were successes. The shelling left many defenders addled, and many easy-to-locate targets—especially shoreside artillery—were pummeled to uselessness. This large-caliber naval gun, for example, was demolished by a direct large-caliber hit. *Official USMC Photo*

Splashes from two direct hits—probably 5-inch rounds—can be seen on this 8-inch naval rifle's armored gun shield. The shield was dented but not penetrated. *Official USMC Photo*

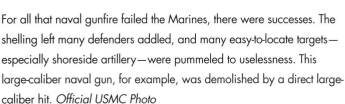

Right: A large-caliber direct hit breached the ammunition stowage for one of the 8-inch naval rifles set up near Betio's southwestern corner. None of the 8-inchers ever got into action because they were obvious targets and received ongoing attention. *Official USMC Photo*

Opposite: A near miss and a direct hit both undermined and smashed open this steel command center. Two of the dead occupants can be seen in the shell crater. Successes like this deflect only slightly the stinging rebuke the architects of the naval gunfire plan deserved and received from their Marine clients. *Official USMC Photo*

continued from page 16

D-DAY

The three battalions of the 2d Marine Regiment (2d Marines) and the 2d Battalion, 8th Marines (2/8); the 1st Battalion, 10th Marines (1/10), a twelve-gun 75mm pack-howitzer battalion; a company of sixteen Sherman M4 medium tanks; the entire reinforced 2d Amphibious Tractor Battalion; the combat engineers of the 1st Battalion, 18th Marines (1/18); the pioneers (shore party) of 2/18; and several special weapons companies armed with 37mm and 75mm anti-tank guns—about six thousand men in all—were awakened aboard their transports at 0300 hours on November 20 and launched into a flurry of activity.

It was not yet light as the first landing boats and Marine-filled amtracs swept out of their holding circles and headed toward the unseen beaches. A destroyer raced toward the shore, spewing 5-inch shells as fast as her gunners could reload.

Dawn brought the first great pillars of smoke to the view of the assault companies. Betio was barely four feet above sea level, only ten feet at its highest point. It would not be seen until the landing boats and amtracs had passed through the first reef.

In the emblematic ritual of the Pacific island-hopping campaign, fully equipped members of the 2d Marines climb down a cargo net from the USS *Biddle* to landing craft waiting beside the ship. *Official USMC Photo*

Landing craft form up near the USS *Heywood*, which has carried 2/8 to Tarawa for its first-wave assault on Red-3. Note that an amtrac is being swayed out from *Heywood's* deck. *Official USMC Photo*

Betio is completely shrouded in smoke as landing craft form up for the final race to the beach. Ahead, in the smoke, Marines aboard 125 amtracs are discovering that there is not enough tide over the reef to allow the follow-on boat waves to approach closer than five hundred yards from the invasion beaches. Note the navy spotter plane near the top of this view. *Official USMC Photo*

Except for .50-caliber machine gunners and the squad leader, the Marines aboard this amtrac—*LVT 45*—have their heads down. *LVT 45* is proceeding as fast as it can—two to four knots—toward Beach Red-3 with a squad of Company E, 2/8, embarked. *Official USMC Photo*

Only the machine gunners have their heads up as *LVT 28* bears down on the left half of Red-3 with a squad of Company F, 2/8, embarked. *Official USMC Photo*

Behind the four infantry assault battalions and their supports, two infantry reserve battalions (1/2 and 3/8) filed into their landing boats. None of these two thousand Marines expected to fight. In fact, 3/8 had been assigned to comb the rubble created by the naval bombardment in search of useful booty and dead bodies to be buried.

Closer to shore, now visible as the minute hand crept toward H-hour and the first wave of amtracs inched across Tarawa lagoon, Marines in the amtracs could see that the giant battleship shells that were still being fired across Betio were exploding harmlessly over water on the far side. The bravado of the navy, which included standing close inshore—more an act of defiance than of

A Marine infantrymen assigned to man one of his amtrac's forward .50-caliber machine guns prepares to open fire at the fast-approaching beach as soon as he has a clear target. Or maybe he will simply spray the seawall as a precaution just before the amtrac touches down. *Official USMC Photo*

LVT 45 is the rightmost amtrac bearing down on Red-3 as it passes the head of Betio's pier, where moments earlier the 2d Marines Scout-and-Sniper Platoon and a platoon of assault engineers cleaned out a few pockets of defenders. By now, *LVT 45* is taking fire from beachside weapons. *Official USMC Photo*

The first amtracs to touch down on Betio did so at 0910, November 20, 1943, along the western half of Beach Red-1. Many other amtracs carrying portions of Battalion Landing Team 3/2 were forced to the right by intense fire from a strongpoint at the juncture of Red-1 and Red-2. The fire was murderous to machine as well as man. There are at least eighteen disabled amtracs in this aerial view of Red-1. *Official USMC Photo*

good gunnery technique—had rendered most of the noisy two-day bombardment ineffective. Had the battleships and cruisers stood farther out and lofted their shells at higher angles of trajectory, there would have been ample destruction. Hardly any large shells had detonated on the island.

Minutes before the first assault waves were due to arrive, two landing boats swept in toward the head of the five-hundred-yard-long pier that ran from the reef surrounding Betio to a point about midway along the island's northern beach. In one boat was the 2d Marines' Scout-and-Sniper Platoon. In the other was a platoon of assault engineers. Their job was to clear Japanese machine gunners from the area, for the pierhead was a perfect place from which to sweep passing amtracs and boats with deadly fire. Several Japanese were found, several TNT charges were set, and then the scouts and engineers jumped back into their boats to follow the lead waves to the beach.

Meanwhile, the first troop-laden tractors had swept to within machine-gun range, and the defenders opened fire, killing or severely wounding many amtrac drivers and causing infantry squads and platoons to become unglued. Many other amtrac

continued on page 35

All the Marines in these two photos were killed as they disembarked from their amtracs on Red-1. They never fired a shot. *Official USMC Photos*

This BARman, killed in a shellhole, probably did engage the defenders before he was shredded by a grenade or mortar round. *Official USMC Photo*

LVT 45 is now halfway along the pier on its way to 2/8's extreme right flank on Beach Red-3. The cluster of buildings to the amtrac's right were set on fire by scouts and engineers as they cleaned out a machine-gun nest that would have hammered *LVT 45*'s human cargo as the tractor drew abreast. *Official USMC Photo*

LVT 45 has stopped at the extreme right side of Red-3. The driver tried and failed to carry his Marines across the seawall, and the tractor has been abandoned by all hands, who have taken cover behind the low seawall. *Official USMC Photo*

continued from page 32

drivers swerved from the fire lanes and sought less-contested routes, though doing so destroyed unit integrity.

The worst surprise of all came when the lead amtracs collided with the reef five hundred yards from shore. This reef was a known quantity, but it was felt there would be enough water over it to float the assault boats of the following waves. The amtracs crossed the reef high and dry, but there was not enough water to float even empty landing craft.

U.S. Navy F6F Hellcat fighter pilots attempted to suppress the Japanese gunners who were by then pouring an increasing volume of fire into the oncoming amtracs, but there was time for only one pass. Then the first Marine ground troops drove ashore.

Three reinforced Marine infantry battalions landed across three beaches on Betio's northern shore. At no point on any of those beaches was it safe for the troops to disembark. Here and there, brave amtrac drivers drove inland to their objectives, but nearly all of the more than fifty vehicles in the first wave stopped at the three-foot-high sea wall; most could not climb over the wall, and where there were breaches in the barrier, the amtracs were disabled by gunfire. The next two assault

As the photographer peeks over the sea-wall, Betio's interior burns fiercely under a bombardment that is just now becoming effective, thanks to on-the-scene reports of its many shortcomings from troops who have now seen up close that the ships and planes have failed them. *Official USMC Photo*

This aerial photo was taken as 2/8 stalled at the seawall. Nearly all the amtracborne assault troops have landed within the western half of Red-3, driven there by intense flanking fire from a wharf marking the beach's eastern extremity. At the top left corner of this view is a stand of palm trees. Within these trees is a huge sand-covered bunker that will stymie 2/8's efforts to advance inland until the third day of the battle. *Official USMC Photo*

waves—seventy-five more amtracs, all there were left in the 2d Marine Division—hit the beach right on time.

As Marine infantrymen immediately vaulted the sides of their amtracs, most were exposed to withering gunfire. Many small-unit leaders were killed or wounded. Immediately, nearly all the survivors hunkered down behind the sea wall—anxious, confused, leaderless. One of the assault companies of 2/2, which landed on the center beach—Red-2—lost five of its six officers within minutes, and one of its platoons was driven hundreds of yards off course, landing at the extreme western tip of the island, where it joined 3/2 on Beach Red-1. The left battalion, 2/8, landed on Beach Red-3 under just slightly less fire and in reasonable organizational condition, but heavy fire from several bunkers right off the beach held these Marines to zero gains.

Fewer than twelve hundred Marines—all infantrymen or combat engineers—landed in the first three waves. Reinforcements and heavier weapons were desperately

This is a captured preinvasion photograph of the southwestern corner of the Red-3 bunker that caused Marines so much trouble. It is the garrison's communications center, and it housed at least one hundred and fifty Japanese combatants when the invasion began. At more than ten feet, it is one of Betio's highest features. *Marine Corps University Archive*

needed. They were on the way—three fresh infantry companies, 81mm mortars, machine guns, and hundreds of special troops. But there was no way to tell them that their shallow-draft landing craft would be unable to breast the reef.

When the first of the landing craft slammed into the reef, navy boat crews dutifully dropped the steel bow ramps, the only protection the Marines had against thousands of bullets that were converging on the dozen or so boats. Those who survived the sheets of fire struggled across the belt of coral that had stopped the boats and jumped off into water that was barely waist deep.

There was absolutely no protection for the wading men of 3/2's follow-on force off Red-1, but most of the men coming to support 2/2 and 2/8 were able to angle toward the pier—which acted as a barrier against most gunfire—and continue on to the beach. There is no way to know how many Marines died in those first shocking minutes after the first wave of landing craft collided with the reef.

Here and there, amtracs that had pulled off the beach after delivering the first waves of troops picked up wounded Marines and carried them to rescue boats beyond the reef. Other amtrackers stopped to pick up the uninjured living who were ducking

continued on page 41

Above and left: The battered remnants of Company F, 2/8, have hunkered down along the seawall within the western half of Red-3. There the lead waves of Marines prepare to make a last stand. As some Marines peer over the seawall, others scavenge machine-gun ammunition from their dead comrades. At some point, an onlooker appears to object to the scavenging and apparently receives a rebuke from a comrade who is gathering belted ammunition. Meanwhile, the other scavenger goes right on with the task at hand. *Official USMC Photos*

Some of the first evacuees are brought back to the beach from small groups that have penetrated to a few yards south of Red-3's seawall. *LVT 23*, which tried and failed to top the seawall, rests at about the center of the occupied half of Red-3 and is positioned to provide good cover for Marines coming and going between the beach and the interior. *Official USMC Photo*

The right extremity of Red-3, marked by a masonry retaining wall, support for the inland end of the pier, is a virtual waste-land of abandoned gear and rubble. Beyond the wall is Red-2, which might as well have been on another planet, for all the battles on either beach affected the other. *Official USMC Photo*

fire on the far side of the reef, and these they carried to the seawall, where hundreds of their comrades had sought cover. Riding an amtrac to the beach was not a free pass, however; dozens more Marines died, and several more amtracs were disabled as they slammed into the incredible volume of fire the defenders were able to pump out.

Here and there, small groups of Marines, some led by officers and noncommissioned officers, but many led by brave privates and privates first class, took control of tiny patches of ground. Few and far between were the organized squads and platoons that found safe passage to shell craters as many as ten or fifteen yards south of the seawall. Most Marines simply huddled behind the seawall.

This landing of the first three reinforced Marine battalions was, for all the heroic exhibitions of very brave men, an unrelieved disaster. Almost as a reflex to adversity, well within the limits of the prudent plan that guided them, the leaders closest to the scene arranged for the reserve battalion to be landed. This unit, 1/2, was sent to the reef by boat. There it rendezvoused with fewer than a dozen amtracs, all that could be gathered at short notice from the shattered 2d Amphibious Tractor Battalion. Several platoons were quickly broken down into squad elements, filled out with a few

continued on page 46

The lead assault waves of 2/2 were brutally handled by Japanese gunners as they closed on Red-2. Five of Company E, 2/2's six officers were killed in minutes, and the company was virtually ineffective as it pulled itself together in the face of such brutality. Many amtracs bearing elements of 2/2 were driven west, to Red-1, by the intensity of fire from the beach boundary strongpoint. At least twenty-five immobilized amtracs can be seen in this D-day aerial photo, but it is possible that a number of these were damaged on second, third, or fourth trips from the reef to the fireswept beach.
Official USMC Photo

LVT 44 became immobilized as it attempted to cross the seawall at what became the western extremity of a truncated Red-2. This amtrac was eventually salvaged and returned to the United States. Today it may be seen in the amphibious vehicle collection at Camp Pendleton, California. *Official USMC Photo*

LVT 44 may be seen in the background of this photo centering on two other immobilized amtracs on Red-2, taken after the battle. *Official USMC Photo*

Many Marines came through the horrendous shock of first contact with Betio's defenders lacking any desire to push ahead against unknown odds. They were willing to defend the toehold, but relatively few were in any shape to advance inland. Their training had been at least temporarily overwhelmed by fire. *Official USMC Photo*

On the other hand, there were Marines among them who could not suppress the desire to forge ahead. Singly, with a buddy or two, or in little ad hoc groups of like-minded strangers, they reset their internal compasses and proceeded to give their all to expand the toehold to a foothold. As some advanced, others died, as seen here. Often, an example of quiet bravery simply shamed other Marines out of the shock that bound them to their places. Even before the shattered assault units found leaders to reorganize them, the dead and wounded flowed north, passed along the way by the newly reinspired on their way south. *Official USMC Photos*

This page and opposite: No plan was needed. It was bitterly obvious that the only realistic course was to unhinge the interlocking Japanese fighting positions by taking out whichever could be taken out, then going on from there to take out the next fighting position, and the next. *Official USMC Photo*

continued from page 38

engineers and machine gunners, and transferred from the boats to the amtracs. Then the boats, which were by then receiving heavy fire, withdrew to a safer distance while the watered-down follow-on assault headed for Red-2 to bolster the immobile 2/2.

There were casualties inflicted upon these reinforcements, but they landed and re-formed, too weak as yet to have an impact upon the battle but relatively unshaken and therefore of use far greater than the larger knots of men who lay disorganized and dis-heartened at their feet. The first serious gains were made in a quick series of jabs that led these men and some members of 2/2 to the edge of the Japanese runway that had first marked Betio as a worthwhile objective.

As the first elements of 1/2 struggled across the seawall, other platoons of the battalion dribbled ashore. Where possible, these newcomers also crossed the seawall, leading still more Marines from 2/2 southward. As the first series of gains were made, Colonel David Shoup, the commander of the 2d Marines—the man in charge of the assault—landed with his staff and one vitally needed command radio, the first to survive the trip to Red-2.

To the right and left, on Beaches Red-1 and Red-3, elements of 3/2 and 2/8 achieved minor gains. Red-1 was isolated from Red-2 by a formidable Japanese

Success bred success, certainly, but there still remained a lethargy of shock that pinned hundreds of Marines behind the fireswept seawall. Here, on the left half of Red-3, the main body of Company F, 2/8, awaits inspiration or the need to defend the beach unto death. The wharf in the background remains a short distance out of Marine hands, but flanking fire from this feature has been neutralized. *Official USMC Photo*

This Marine will probably never get to his feet to take part in the fierce fight for Betio. Consider this: his photo is being taken by a fellow Marine, standing tall, armed with a camera. *Official USMC Photo*

strongpoint, and there were not enough Marines on either Red-1 or Red-2 to reduce the strongpoint or to link up. On Red-3, 2/8 was in physical contact with the troops on Red-2, but it also faced an extremely formidable defensive network right at the edge of the seawall. Gains on Red-3 were measured in feet.

Each of the dwindling number of amtracs that reached Red-2 brought in about a dozen fresh Marines. Of each dozen, an average of six quickly became casualties or sought cover behind the seawall. But the remaining six climbed warily over the seawall and ran, rolled, or crawled across the fine coral sand and mixed debris to holes or to the wrecks of buildings and bunkers that could be defended and used as way stations for additional small advances southward.

As soon as Colonel Shoup could make an assessment of the awful situation on the beach, he asked that 3/8, the division reserve, be landed to support 2/8 on Red-3. The fresh battalion was mounted in about a dozen personnel boats and tank lighters, but no one told its officers about the reef barrier, and no one sent amtracs to meet it. As with the follow-up companies of the lead battalions, the unsuspecting troops of 3/8 were shocked to the soles of their feet when their boats slammed into the reef.

Ramps were dropped, and Marines dutifully stepped into the withering Japanese gunfire. Dozens of Marines died in the boats and atop the reef. Hundreds, however, sidestepped to the pier, an angling walk of several hundred yards for many of them. Hundreds of weapons, packs, helmets, radios, and mortar rounds were dropped into the lagoon, the better to gain survival in the waist-deep water.

Several hundred members of 3/8 stopped at the pierhead to catch a collective breath. Hundreds more waded to the beach on one side or another of the pier. Of these, hundreds hunkered down behind the seawall. And of those few who entered the fight beside the bloodied companies of 2/8, only a few dozen were in gaggles that could be called organized. The first reinforcements from 3/8 to reach Red-3 helped take a little ground, but they had no major impact.

continued on page 50

Following the amtrac-mounted assault waves to Betio were the assault battalions' tactical reserve—more rifle squads, light machine guns, 60mm mortars, and assault engineers, all loaded into LCVPs and a few larger LCMs. Farther out, awaiting orders to land, were battalion commanders and alternate command groups led by the battalion executive officers; battalion communications teams; such battalion assets as 81mm mortars, medium machine guns, and battalion aid stations; and attached units that included more engineers, pioneer detachments, and other attachments along the lines of artillery and naval gunfire observer teams. These units were also mounted in LCVPs and LCMs. Subject to each assault battalion commander's whims, the battalion command posts and support units started for the beach earlier or later. Only on Red-3 was the battalion commander, Major Henry "Jim" Crowe, able to reach his command. The 2/2 commanding officer was killed by a Japanese machine gun, and the executive officer was driven to Red-1 by heavy fire. The 3/2 commander and executive officer failed to land at all, so the battalion weapons company commander took charge of Red-1 and its amalgam of Marines from 3/2 and 2/2. On Red-2, at length, an observer, a lieutenant colonel from the 4th Marine Division staff, took control of the troops. When 1/2 landed on Red-2, its commander, a major, fell under the observer's command. *Official USMC Photo*

It was bad enough that Marines who reached the reef in landing craft had to alight and wade to the beach in water between knee- and neck-high, but the trip was made ever so much more dangerous by fire from this wreck, a schooner that had been run aground on the reef by her British master when Betio fell to the Japanese in December 1941. Warships tried to hit the hulk, which sat about a hundred yards west of the pierhead, but they were unable to quiet her. Finally, an air strike was called. *Official USMC Photo*

With or without the hulk's machine guns in play, brave men waded resolutely through the lagoon from reef to pier. This is what Betio looked like on D-day to men whose first clear view came as the bow ramps dropped in front of them. *Official USMC Photo*

Everyone in Betio lagoon was free to try any path to shore that seemed to work. Two Marines who tried to rush south from the pierhead were eventually shot dead. *Official USMC Photo*

continued from page 47

There was only one uncommitted infantry battalion remaining under operational control of the 2d Marine Division, 1/8. The 6th Marines was steaming in circles near Betio, but it was the V Marine Amphibious Corps (VMAC) force reserve, as likely to be sent to support the 27th Infantry Division's bid for Makin Atoll, well to the north of Tarawa, as to Betio. Until the 6th Marines could be released by the force commander, the 2d Marine Division would have to exercise extreme caution in the commitment of its last meaningful asset.

Of the three beaches, Red-1 was the most isolated. The bulk of 3/2 was probing outward from a small but secure perimeter it had established early on around the northwestern tip of the island. It did not seem worthwhile to reinforce Red-1 because the situation was fairly stable and because there was nowhere to go even if the objective was taken in its entirety.

The surviving portions of 1/2 and 2/2, as well as the regimental headquarters, were on Red-2, the center beach. These units had a chance to take ground to the south, so Red-2 seemed a likely place to land 1/8. So did Red-3. The initial assault battalion there, 2/8, was fairly well organized and, though it was meeting fierce opposition from formidable defensive emplacements, its prospects were fairly bright. One

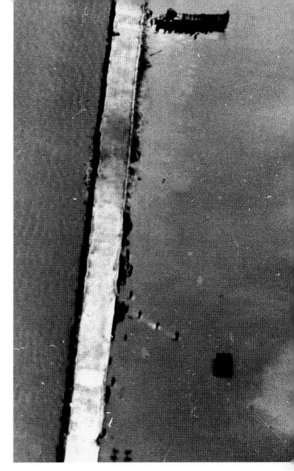

Wading alongside the pier was a mixed blessing, as one could still draw fire from Japanese guns positioned far to the flank, but the notion of protection seemed to lure most men toward the pier. The western side of the structure was paralleled by a small-boat channel, which meant it was possible to go in over your head. A landing craft that attempted passage to the beach via the channel ran aground and was knocked sideways, thus providing a protected way station for waders in need of a rest. Thousands of Marines passed this way on D-day and D+1. *Official USMC Photos*

Shortly after Red-2 was struck, someone heaved a satchel charge through an opening in a nondescript building at the base of the pier, on the Red-2 side. This powerful explosive charge detonated the contents of the building, which turned out to be the dump for aerial torpedoes for Japanese aircraft based on Betio. The ground shook across the island and lagoon, and a huge geyser of smoke and debris was visible to anyone who was looking in that direction from even miles away. It is not known how many people were vaporized, or even injured, in the calamity. *Official USMC Photo*

By the time 3/8 began to stream ashore, the debris at the torpedo dump had settled, and it and an adjacent masonry bathhouse were used as protected way stations for late arrivals who could not find it in themselves to join the fight quite yet. *Official USMC Photo*

factor favoring a landing by 1/8 on Red-3 was that the 8th Marines headquarters could then control all three of its own infantry battalions in a definable area. Whether for this or for better reasons, it was decided to land 1/8 on Red-3, behind 2/8 and 3/8. But it was not to be. Communications difficulties and an error by an aerial observer kept 1/8 circling offshore all night.

D-day at Betio ended with more than nine thousand Marines committed to the fight. Hundreds had died or been gravely injured just trying to get to the tiny rim of beach. Four of 1/10's 75mm pack howitzers had been landed, as had two 75mm half-tracks and four medium tanks. There also were a few 37mm antitank guns ashore. No objectives worth mentioning had been secured.

Above: If every newly arrived group of Marines lost strength and momentum when some men dropped out of the fight for at least brief rest breaks, the battle lines were nonetheless bolstered by men who had not the heart to even rest, and by those who rested, found their resolve, and joined the fight. *Official USMC Photo*

Left: Ever so slowly, order emerged from chaos. Here, a wire team runs a line along Red-3, the better to organize and control even so shocked and battered a modern military force as the amalgam of 2/8 and 3/8. *Official USMC Photo*

D-day: Taking Stock

Most of the men who had survived the trip to the beaches were demoralized, and nearly all of them were huddled behind the seawall or under cover in shell and bomb craters. For the most part they were unable to organize themselves into combat units and advance.

Ammunition, food, water, and medical supplies were not getting to the beaches, though brave sailors and Marines risked life and limb to run boatloads of goods to the pierhead, which was as close as they could get. There were not nearly enough amtracs left to evacuate the wounded, bring in fresh troops, land artillery, and carry supplies from the pierhead to the beaches. Yet all of these things were done by the incredibly brave amtrackers.

continued on page 67

Recognized throughout the Marine Corps as simply a force of nature, 2/8's commanding officer, Major Jim Crowe, had risen from the ranks to serve as warrant officer at Guadalcanal, and then to junior major in command of one of the three assault battalions going ashore at Betio. As soon as Crowe reached Red-3, the narrow, embattled toehold was considered by one and all to be well in hand. Tireless, inspiring, loud, profane, a tactical genius, and much more, Crowe quickly assessed what he had to work with, then worked with it. Seen here with a handset to his ear, multitasking to beat the band, Crowe established his command post behind *LVT 23*, at the center of his domain, and aggressively went after the enemy on his doorstep. Along the way, he inspired everyone within eyeball range and earshot. *Official USMC Photo*

Colonel Dave Shoup, the 2d Marines commanding officer, had been spot-promoted to his current rank while at sea on the way to Tarawa. He replaced an older man who was too ill to command. As division operations officer, he had written the Tarawa invasion plan. Though he had less time in grade than any other colonel in the division, no one questioned his elevation to command of the assault force. He went ashore at the first opportunity on D-day morning, wrenching his knee painfully on the way and, as had Jim Crowe on Red-3, began winning the battle for Betio quite simply by working harder and smarter than anyone else in the world could have done. Seen here at the end of the battle, Shoup is resting his weight on the bicycle to relieve pressure on his untended wrenched knee. He was awarded one of Tarawa's four Medals of Honor for his unremitting heroic effort—the only one pinned on a living Marine. Twenty years later, Shoup was deep selected to serve as commandant of the Marine Corps. *Official USMC Photo*

Close behind Colonel Shoup's accession of command ashore, 2d Marines communicators were able to get all the components of a field radio ashore, thus providing the commander with the means to speak directly to superiors aboard the USS *Maryland*, the fleet flagship, as well as some subordinate commanders ashore.
Official USMC Photo

Above: Once Colonel Shoup had a command radio at his disposal, he ordered Weapons Company, 2d Marines, and part of Weapons Company, 8th Marines, to land 75mm halftracks and 37mm antitank guns on Red-2 and Red-3. The landing craft embarking one halftrack was sunk on its away to the beach, but the other halftrack and the 37mm guns were all disembarked at the reef or pierhead. One lucky jeep driver drove the 37mm in his care all the way to the beach via the pier. Shown here is a 37mm crew manhandling its weapon and ammunition alongside the pier. Even the one 75mm halftrack was of immeasurable value in expanding Red-2, and the 37s, though rather puny, materially affected the ability of Marines on both beaches to reduce some Japanese bunkers and pillboxes. *Official USMC Photo*

Opposite: All sixteen M4 Sherman medium tanks on loan to the 2d Marine Division from Company C, I Marine Amphibious Corps Tank Battalion, were routinely unloaded and sent ashore, one five-tank platoon per beach. These were the first Marine Shermans ever committed to combat. Several were lost in deep shell craters on the way to the beach and through other mishaps—running blindly into a burning fuel dump, for example. One tank was severely damaged when it was bombed by a friendly carrier plane. In the end, all five tanks committed to Red-2 were disabled; all but two of six committed to Red-1 were disabled; and one tank—*Colorado*, seen here—survived D-day battles ashore on Red-3, even though it was hit and set on fire by a Japanese antitank round. *Official USMC Photo*

Above: The battle for the interior continued in fits and starts throughout D-day. Seen here are two light machine gunners on their way inland from the cover of Red-3's command post marker, *LVT 23*. A Marine who was killed in a bid to cross the seawall still lies where he died, but the machine gunners studiously avoid looking at him as the leader gauges when it will be best to make his bid. *Official USMC Photo*

Right: As many Marines stick behind the cover of the Red-3 seawall as cross it. *Official USMC Photo*

Left: Among the willing combatants below Red-3 were two flamethrower assaultmen who left a wide swath of burning bunkers and charred Japanese corpses. Horrible to look at—and smell—these visible Japanese dead raised morale for all Marines who view them. *Official USMC Photo*

Below: Ever so slowly, ever so methodically, Marines achieve a rhythm of mayhem that overwhelms one Japanese fighting position after another. Here, below Red-3, the crew of a 13mm antiaircraft machine gun—an efficient killer of ground troops—has been shot to death around its stanchion-mounted weapon. *Official USMC Photo*

By day's end, elements of 2/8 and 3/8 have reached the wide, open expanse of the airfield taxiway. There they decide to dig in for the night and hope that heavy weapons will be forthcoming to support an assault across the open ground. *Official USMC Photo*

Opposite: All along the occupied portion of Red-2, survivors of 2/2 and 1/2 push inland to gain breathing room and deliver themselves from intense, deadly fire that has hemmed them in and picked them off for hours. Early on, the Marines who advance do so as individuals who have to locate their own inspiration. But their example shakes many onlookers from their postlanding lethargy and sends them forward as well. Finally, tough, old Marine staff noncommissioned officers who grow embarrassed by the partial commitment to fight get junior Marines not long out of boot camp on their way south via the loud, cadenced order and oath that accompanied their ascension to the right to claim the title of United States Marines. *Official USMC Photos*

Three officers study the battlefield south of Red-2. As officers with battlefield experience and command authority make their way to the focal point of the Marine organization on Red-2, more can be put to the useful work of gathering information and observations from which an integrated plan can be ironed out, at least for crossing Betio from Beach Red-2 to Beach Black-2. Initially hit-or-miss in its organization and indiscriminate in its application, the combat potential that is ashore on Red-2 suddenly congeals under good, assertive leadership and makes ready to carry out an actual plan put in place by seasoned planners. *Official USMC Photo*

Opposite: The photographer captures a small unit of Marines as it thunders south from Red-2 across some open ground. The immediate objective is a way station where the troops can catch their breath and get some advice from a spotter who has the next rush planned out. *Official USMC Photos*

Above and right: After clearing out a bunker housing a Japanese aid station, Marines on their way south from Red-2 are confronted with a formidable obstacle—the wide, flat, completely open coral-topped runway that presents a clear shot for hundreds of yards to east and west. This is where about 150 Marines organized into an ad hoc company were ordered to dig in for the first night ashore. *Official USMC Photo*

Left and below: Better organized and integrated but far weaker in numbers, the main body of 3/2 on isolated Red-1 took the entire day to spread slowly southward along Beach Green. Many Japanese positions were blotted out during aggressive attacks, and one patrol, as seen here, got nearly to the Japanese 8-inch battery on Betio's southwestern point. But small numbers and justifiable worries about a night counterattack caused the battalion-size force to fall back to a defensible perimeter, deep but compact, around Betio's northwestern point. *Official USMC Photos*

Late on D-day afternoon, the commanding officer of 1/10, a twelve-gun 75mm pack howitzer battery, decided on his own authority to land part of his battalion on Red-2. There was a great deal of confusion and not many good ways to get the howitzers ashore, but in the end two 75s were broken down and carried ashore in amtracs, and three more were unloaded at the pierhead, broken down, and carried to Red-2 in the dark by their crews. Shown here, an amtrac with a gun crew aboard tows a 75mm howitzer from a landing boat toward the pierhead. *Official USMC Photo*

As soon as his troops ashore were operating under competent command and an authentic battle plan, Colonel Dave Shoup ordered that the dead be gathered up from the battlefield to be interred in makeshift graves. This was a health measure, certainly, but it was really aimed at lifting the immense drag on morale that the dead bodies of comrades have upon the living. *Official USMC Photo*

D+1

It was finally learned at the 2d Marine Division command post (colocated with the VMAC command post aboard the battleship *Maryland*) in the wee hours of D+1—November 21—that 1/8 had not yet landed on Red-3. Given this opportunity to rethink his earlier decision, the division commander ordered the fresh battalion to Red-2, the center beach. It was by then clear that the deepest D-day penetrations and thus the best chance of ultimate success resided there. Before it was decided to land 1/8, however, the proposition that all the shattered battalions already on Betio be evacuated was debated—and rejected.

For unknown reasons, 1/8 was not informed of the deadly problem at the reef. Nor were amtracs collected to carry the fresh troops in. Well after sunrise, in plain view of thousands of horrified Marines and pleased Japanese, the landing craft in which 1/8 Marines had spent nearly a full day slammed into the reef along several hundred yards of frontage five hundred yards from Red-2. The boat crews dutifully dropped their ramps, and the dutiful Marines jumped into the water and walked upright across the exposed reef before wading into the waist-deep lagoon. Japanese machine gunners shot 1/8 to ribbons.

The survivors of the battalion (Company A, for example, mustered fewer than seventy effectives on the beach, down from two hundred) formed up on the right flank of Red-2 and, with bits and parts of other units, swung over to the attack. They ground slowly into the clustered bunkers and pillboxes that barred the way to Red-1 and a linkup with isolated 3/2. This single attack by the shattered battalion ranks among the bravest of undertakings in all the annals of all the wars recorded by man, yet few actions have gone so long unsung.

continued on page 73

One of the first orders of business on November 21 was getting 1/8 ashore on Red-2. The battalion had been moving through Tarawa lagoon for nearly a full day when the order arrived, but the troops knew nothing about having to wade five hundred yards from the reef to the beach. Many were killed or wounded by machine guns still active in the strongpoint at the boundary of Red-1 and Red-2. As soon as the survivors had re-formed ashore, they were dispatched to reduce the strongpoint. *Official USMC Photo*

This page and opposite: Another early order of business on D+2 was getting a grip on the flow of supplies to Red-2 and Red-3. Unable to work across the reef, the entire effort defaulted to the pierhead, where authority took most of D-day to emerge. But order and an organization were eventually imposed. Supply-laden landing craft were inspected before being allowed to touch down at the pierhead, supplies were sorted and stowed as space allowed, porters were dragooned from among Marines heading to the beach, and the weight-bearing structure was shored up as needed. *Official USMC Photos*

Pages 70–73: Efficient medical evacuation also came together on D+2, when reliable means were dedicated to getting wounded Marines from the beach to the reef and then to transports equipped with medical suites. Fully functioning aid stations were established on the beaches to stabilize and sort the wounded; rubber rafts and amtracs working between the beaches and the reef were assigned hospital corpsmen; and small craft with corpsmen aboard carried the wounded out to the ships. *Official USMC Photos*

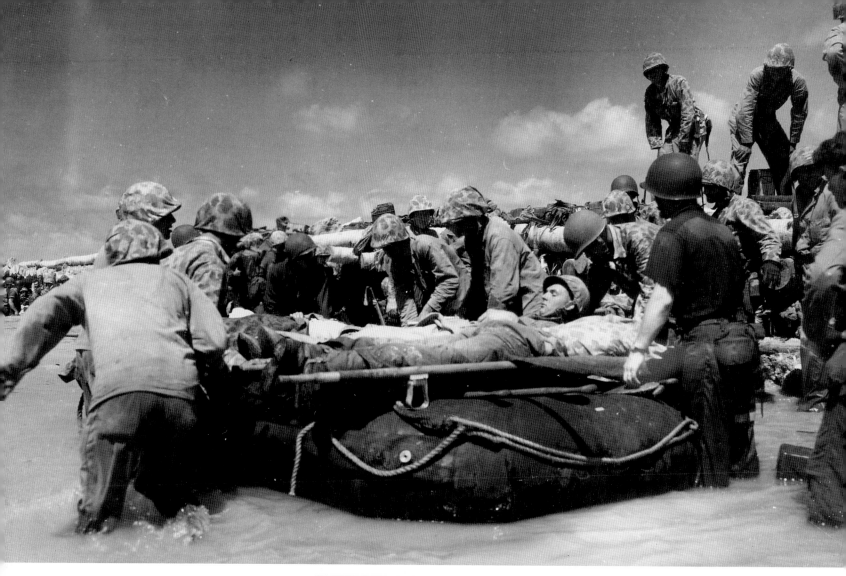

continued from page 67

Even as 1/8 was cut to ribbons, what remained of 3/2 attacked southward from its enclave on Red-1. Support was provided by several U.S. Navy destroyers standing offshore and two medium tanks, of which only one had a 75mm main gun in working order. In hours of bitter fighting, the battalion reached the southern shore. By clearing the western beach—Beach Green—the attack provided a safe access to Betio.

As 3/2 took ground south of Red-1, elements of 1/2 and 2/2 reached the southern beach opposite Red-2. Opposition on the ground between these beaches did not cease, and both flanks remained dangerously exposed, but small groups of Marines were fed southward to secure the large stretches of open ground that provided haven for dozens and perhaps hundreds of Japanese snipers.

There were also modest gains on Red-3 during D+1. A great deal of time and effort went into organizing 2/8's stable line and reorganizing 3/8 from the hundreds of D-day dropouts who reported for duty on D+1. Mostly, the two battalions on Red-3 consolidated their meager gains and edged closer to several formidable strongpoints the Japanese doggedly manned within spitting distance of the seawall. Gains were modest on Red-3 this day, but plenty of Japanese died, and some key ground was taken.

The 6th Marines was released to the 2d Marine Division's operational control late in the morning. It was decided to land 1/6 on Beach Green and send it into the attack down the island's long axis. Meanwhile, 2/6 was to land on the adjacent island, Bairiki, to cut the Japanese line of retreat and provide security for 2/10's dozen 75mm pack howitzers. Once on Bairiki, the howitzer and infantry battalions would have the Japanese on Betio boxed in.

At 1706 hours on November 21, Colonel Shoup was asked by the division command post to file a situation report. His reply was: "Casualties, many; percentage dead not known. Combat Efficiency: We are winning."

It turned out that 1/6 could not be landed on Beach Green until very late on D+1. The division commander therefore decided to delay the battalion's ground attack until daylight.

continued on page 82

The battle to expand the beachheads began at first light and stretched through the entire day. Some of the task on Red-2 and Red-3 was made easier by the availability of, at first, five of 1/10's 75mm pack howitzers on Red-2. The gunners answered every call even though they spent the early part of the day under intermittent small-arms fire. As well, U.S. Navy destroyers provided pinpoint on-call gunnery as needed. *Official USMC Photo*

This 60mm mortar, set up on Red-3, gamely fulfilled any requests for fire support that came its way, but its rounds were unable to breach any of the fighting positions the Japanese were manning. *Official USMC Photo*

Eight 2d Tank Battalion M3 light tanks were ashore during the course of D+2. Their 37mm guns were unable to penetrate many Japanese bunkers and pillboxes, but the tanks answered all calls and acted as moving cover when Marines had to cross open spaces, particularly the main runway south of Red-2. In the background here is a log airplane revetment, which the tanks used as a base. *Official USMC Photo*

This Marine was shot dead on the main runway as he advanced south toward Beach Black-2. Tread marks left by at least one light tank can be seen on the runway's crushed coral surface. *Official USMC Photo*

These Marines are checking on Japanese defenses along Black-2 before they commit themselves to moving from cover. *Official USMC Photo*

Dozens of Marines from 1/2 and 2/2 reached this antitank ditch just short of Black-2, but they could not quite hold the beach itself. By nightfall on D+2, supplies and reinforcements had been pushed through to make the occupation of the ditch and adjacent structures permanent. *Official USMC Photo*

Most Marines on Red-3 remained mired in local fighting close to the beach. The confluence of the main runway and a taxiway constrained the advance to the south, and several large bunkers and numerous outlying positions hemmed in the beachhead to the east. *Official USMC Photo*

This page and opposite: For all that they were hemmed in on D+2, elements of 2/8 and 3/8 managed to take ground and consolidate their position. Here, an ad hoc unit of Marines moves on a cluster of active pillboxes. In the first photo, the leader or an alert observer points out an objective as fellow Marines advance into position. In the second photo, Marines take cover behind a neutralized pillbox while a flamethrower team reduces a position farther on. Note the thick black smoke. *Official USMC Photos*

This pillbox is being demolished by TNT blocks placed by a team of assault engineers. *Official USMC Photo*

On isolated Red-1, 3/2 and stragglers from 2/2 attacked behind two medium tanks to take a ribbon of ground along Beach Green all the way to Beach Black-1. As soon as Beach Green was completely in Marine hands, defensive positions were established to the east, and the tricky job of mopping up the jumbled Japanese defenses began. The Marine shown here is firing into a Japanese soldier who already lies dead in the entryway to the bunker in the center of the photo. *Official USMC Photo*

Beginning at 1845 hours on D+2, 1/6 and its supports began to come ashore on Beach Green. The reinforced battalion was the first Marine command to land on Betio without taking casualties. Briefed to undertake an attack from west to east down the long axis of the island, 1/6 arrived too late to begin, so it manned the front line screening Beach Green and prepared to step off early on D+2. *Official USMC Photo*

For all the progress various elements of the 2d Marine Division made on D+1, the leftmost wing of the invasion force, in the eastern half of occupied Red-3, was unable to take ground because the two largest bunkers on the island and a host of formidable outlying emplacements stood in the way. Shown here, Company F, 2/8, has been stalled at the seawall since its D-day storm landing. By dawn on D+2, 2/8 and 3/8 and their supports were ready to take on the entire defensive array that blocked Red-3. *Official USMC Photo*

D+2

November 22, 1943—D+2—was the best day the 2d Marine Division had at Tarawa; it was the day the Japanese lost their grip. Mounting its assault down the long axis of the tiny island, the fully intact 1/6 met up with parts of the other units that had struggled inland from Red-1 and Red-2 on D-day and D+1. Behind 1/6's steady advance, growing portions of 1/2 and 2/2 scoured the area between the northern and southern beaches, eradicating Japanese snipers wherever they could be located. At the boundary of Red-1 and Red-2, facing the intensely defended beach-boundary strongpoint, 3/2 was assigned to help 1/8 clear the sector. Both units pushed slowly into the built-up area from two sides. In time the two weary, undermanned battalions linked up and pressed upon the strongpoint from three sides. Their backs to the sea with no chance of retreat, the Japanese here presented an even more formidable stand, if that was possible.

The two battalions on Red-3—2/8 and 3/8—also made significant gains on D+2. The key to the Japanese defense was a huge covered bunker barely ten yards south of the seawall. (If 10 yards seems a piddling distance, consider that these

continued on page 85

First there was an attack by U.S. Navy F6F Hellcats aimed at keeping Japanese heads down just beyond 2/8's left flank. Then the lone surviving tank on Red-3 moved in behind Company F, 2/8, to blast several fighting positions near the wharf that marked the eastern extremity of the Marine line. *Official USMC Photos*

Closer to the center of Company F, 2/8's seawall line, a mixed force of assault engineers, pioneers, and riflemen that had been organized over two days by pioneer 1st Lieutenant Alexander Bonnyman mounted a coordinated attack on the central feature in the Japanese defensive zone, the immense covered communications bunker. Seen here, Marines under Bonnyman's command rush the bunker from the west, just inland from the seawall. The third Marine from the left is armed with a flamethrower. *Official USMC Photo*

Marines who have been immobilized for two days emerge from cover to join the rush. *Official USMC Photo*

As the main body lunges toward the top of the bunker, Lieutenant Bonnyman, in the lead, almost single-handedly stalls a Japanese counterattack from within the bunker. The main body reaches the summit in time to turn the Japanese back, but not before Bonnyman is shot dead. He will later be awarded a posthumous Medal of Honor. *Official USMC Photo*

Below: First Lieutenant Alexander Bonnyman Jr., Company C, 1st Battalion, 18th Marines. *Marine Corps University Archive*

two battalions had been crammed into a perimeter seventy-five yards wide by twenty yards at its deepest point for two full days.) D+1 had seen the destruction of several outlying pillboxes and bunkers, but the key to the main bunker was finally turned by a tiny group of engineers and pioneers. A flamethrower that was fired down a ventilator shaft forced all the Japanese to evacuate the structure. They ran directly into the fire of the last Sherman tank on Red-3, and nearly a hundred were killed in the open, the most Japanese anyone on Red-3 saw at one time during the entire battle.

The fall of the covered bunker allowed 2/8 and 3/8 to re-form into battalion tactical units. While most of 3/8 cleared ground south of the beach, 2/8 attacked eastward and soon reduced a second huge concrete bunker, the island command post. As soon as the Japanese command bunker fell, 2/8 dug in and sent platoons and squads to the rear to pry out the plague of snipers it had left in its wake.

All through D+2, as the 2d and 8th Marines took ground along the beaches, 1/6 advanced steadily up Betio's long axis against minor opposition. There were a few big fights at several large strongpoints, but casualties were light and gains were substantial. Finally, 1/6 stopped in line with 2/8's farthest advance and dug in for the night. By then, 3/6 had been landed on Beach Green and had come up to support the advance.

continued on page 89

Japanese fleeing eastward from the communications bunker toward the island command bunker were mowed down in the open by Marine infantrymen and the lone medium tank. *Official USMC Photo*

The command bunker, east of the extremity of Marine holding on Red-3, was struck repeatedly by large-caliber naval shells for five long days, but there were no breaches in the walls. The leading elements of Marines to reach the bunker on D+2 were stymied by its sheer power until a flamethrower assaultman stepped through the partially opened front door and doused the interior. The bunker fell in short order, and the Marines advanced to take nearly the entire length of the Red-3 zone as far south as the wide, open airfield turning circle. *Official USMC Photo*

Throughout the island on D+2, at the front and behind the lines, Marines worked diligently to kill the defenders in place. Shown here, Marines cover a Japanese position with small arms as an engineer bulldozer entombs the occupants, living or dead, with tons of sand. *Official USMC Photo*

At a moment no one especially noticed, what had been a palpable defensive spirit simply evaporated, transforming the bulk of Betio's diehard defenders to the status of stragglers. *Official USMC Photo*

As 1/8 pressed in from the east against the beach boundary strongpoint between Red-2 and Red-1, the reorganized main body of 3/2 pressed in from the west with an assist from one medium tank and at least one 75mm halftrack. Progress through D+2 was good, but a tough core of defenders remained in place at nightfall. *Official USMC Photo*

During the latter half of D+2, Marines throughout the expanding beachhead were reporting the increasing frequency of Japanese suicides. *Official USMC Photo*

The ultimate suicidal act was the assault against 1/6's night-defense line across most of Betio in line with the airfield turning circle. The Japanese were fixed by 1/6's infantry weapons and pulverized by unremitting fire support from destroyers on both flanks and 2/10's 75mm pack howitzers in the rear, on neighboring Bairiki Island. *Official USMC Photo*

continued from page 85

D+3

The Japanese lost it that night. Although the ultimate outcome of the battle for Betio had passed beyond doubt, grave harm might have been inflicted on the attackers if the defenders had remained hunkered down to fight from well-built fighting positions in the narrow, relatively untouched eastern tail of the island, where the Marines would have to advance on an extremely narrow front. But five hundred able-bodied Japanese assaulted dug-in 1/6 during the night. Massed infantry weapons combined with supporting fire from several destroyers offshore and 2/10's pack howitzers on Bairiki doomed the Japanese assault at its outset. The fight was tough, and casualties among the Marine defenders were heavy, but nearly all the Japanese left on Betio at sunset were dead by sunrise.

Betio was declared secure at 1305 hours, November 23, 1943, following a relatively bloodless sweep of the eastern tail of the island by 3/6. Just before this fresh battalion attained its goal, the last organized resistance facing 3/2 and 1/8 was overcome at the beach-boundary strongpoint. Snipers, many of them badly wounded men in blasted buildings all across Betio, held out for days, taking a toll on combat Marines and the technicians who followed them closely to rehabilitate and expand Betio's airfield.

In just seventy-six hours, almost to the minute, all but 13 Japanese servicemen and all but 134 Korean and Okinawan laborers who had garrisoned Betio were dead. So were more than six hundred U.S. Marines and sailors.

Tarawa was a victory—of that there is no doubt. In the best sense, it was a stunning defeat of unremitting adversity by brave men—a victory at its fullest.

Following 3/6's almost bloodless advance down the long axis of Betio's eastern tail, the job of taking stock began. Shown here, one of a very few Japanese captives is interrogated by two Marine luminaries. At far right is Lieutenant Colonel Evans Carlson, the former Marine Raider commander, who is serving as a 4th Marine Division observer. Carlson has played a pivotal role in assisting Colonel Dave Shoup ashore. Next to Carlson, with binoculars, is another former Raider commander, Colonel Merritt Edson, now the 2d Marine Division chief of staff. *Official USMC Photo*

Right: As Marine and navy senior commanders fan out across Betio to attend briefings and have their photos taken for posterity, this battle survivor is thinking about his next meal. Several barnyard animals survived the battle; a duck was taken in as a pet, the rest were eaten. *Official USMC Photo*

Below: Official USMC Photo

Official USMC Photo

For the first time in the Pacific War, Marines landed behind an adequate, effective naval and air bombardment. *Official U.S. Navy Photo*

CHAPTER 2

The Marshall Islands

PLANNING AND PREPARATIONS

The invasion of Kwajalein Atoll in the Japanese-mandated Marshall Islands was a smash-and-grab operation very much like the November 1943 assault on Tarawa, only easier. After Tarawa and Makin the next logical step toward the goal of mutually supporting airfields across the central Pacific was the Marshall Islands, where ready-made airfields awaited. In addition to a superb fleet anchorage off Kwajalein Island, Kwajalein Atoll—540 miles northwest of Tarawa—had special significance for Marines who recalled that the Japanese land-based bombers that had smashed Wake Island at the start of the Pacific War had operated from Roi Airdrome, also in Kwajalein Atoll.

Following months of staff work, the invasion was set for January 29, 1944. The new, untested 4th Marine Division was to assault Roi and its sandspit-connected twin, Namur; the U.S. Army's 7th Infantry Division was to assault Kwajalein Island; and an army regimental combat team was to seize the largely undefended fleet anchorage in Majuro Atoll. Two main improvements on the Tarawa plan that were to be employed at Kwajalein were longer, harder-hitting naval and air bombardments and the emplacement of artillery on outlying islands ahead of the main show against Kwajalein, Roi, and Namur. Several neat innovations included the conversion of a flotilla of LCIs to fire 4.5-inch rockets—LCI(R)s—and the inaugural use of amtracs rigged out as armored amphibious tanks—LVT(A)s—each carrying a 37mm gun and bristling with five machine guns.

In December 1943, Army Air Forces bombers based on fields in the Gilbert Islands, U.S. Navy carrier aircraft, and U.S. Navy surface bombardment forces began the systematic interdiction of bases in the Marshalls—both the projected targets of amphibious assaults and bases from which the targets might be supported, including Wake Island.

Roi and Namur were thought to be defended by an even greater force than the one that had so bloodily defended Betio, but they were not. Only eighteen hundred to twenty-six hundred combat troops were deployed on the islands, and they manned fewer and less-well-emplaced defense positions.

continued on page 97

Roi's airfield was pounded to rubble by the warships and finished off by bombs and rockets delivered by carrier bombers and fighters. *Official USMC Photo*

This reinforced concrete pillbox on Namur was struck dead on its firing embrasure by a naval shell. *Official USMC Photo*

Aerial bombs took out the two round structures in this view, and a naval shell or aerial rocket breached the bunker at right. *Official USMC Photo*

At least forty Japanese were killed when Namur's administration center was pulverized by large-caliber naval shells and bombs. *Official USMC Photo*

continued from page 93

PRELIMINARIES

Beginning at dawn on January 31, 1944, the 25th Marines, carried by V Marine Amphibious Corps' 10th Amphibian Tractor Battalion and bolstered by Company A, 1st Armored Amphibian Tractor Battalion, as well as divisional combat support units, assaulted five small islands from which 75mm pack howitzers and 105mm field howitzers of the 14th Marines would outflank the defenses on Roi and Namur. High winds and heavy seas delayed the assault, but the lead waves carried on, with LCI gunboats—LCI(G)s—and LVT(A)s ahead to deliver final suppressive fire. Carrier fighters also suppressed the defenses until the last possible moment.

At 0952, Company B, 1/25, was the first American unit to land on pre-war Japanese territory, Ennuebing Island. Thereafter, other elements of 1/25 swept over Mellu Island. Thirty Japanese corpses were eventually unearthed, and five prisoners were taken. Shortly, 3/14 landed its 75mm pack howitzers on Ennuebing from LVTs, and 4/14's 105mm howitzers landed from landing craft on Mellu. Two more artillery outposts were secured by 2/25 during the afternoon, and 1/14 and 2/14 quickly landed their 75mm pack howitzers. A fifth outlying island was secured late in the day by 3/25 despite terrible weather-related problems, and an ad hoc gunfire force of five 75mm halftracks, seventeen 37mm guns, four 81mm mortars, nine 60mm mortars, and sixty-one machine guns was set up on the side of the island facing Namur, which was only four hundred yards away. The seizure of all five D-day objectives came at the cost of just one Marine wounded, by a friendly strafer.

LCVPs circle as they await their turn to embark Marines from this transport. A destroyer is seen to the right. *Official USMC Photo*

Amtracs loaded with members of the 25th Marines circle near a U.S. Navy cruiser on January 31 before moving on the small islands around Roi and Namur. *Official USMC Photo*

Marine armored amtracs—LCT(A)s—made their combat debut on January 31, 1944. They were armed with a 37mm gun and five machine guns. *Official USMC Photo*

INVASION

As amtracs completed the work of carrying the 25th and 14th Marines ashore, they were to climb aboard LSTs for a night refueling. The idea was to use the LSTs to transfer invasion troops from the transports and carry them close to the shore in the morning, then launch them in orderly groups of amtracs. But the D-day operations took longer to complete than was foreseen, so most 10th Amphibian Tractor Battalion amtracs did not get to the LST area until dusk or later. On the one hand, the amtrac crews couldn't find their assigned LSTs, and on the other hand, many picky LST commanders refused to take aboard or refuel amtracs that hadn't been assigned to their ships. The result was chaos and a lot of fuel-starved amtracs that were supposed to lift the 24th Marines to Namur. On top of that, it was extremely difficult and time-consuming to transfer amtracs from an LST's weather deck to the tank deck—which is what most of the 4th Amphibian Tractor Battalion needed to do to get the 23d Marines ashore on Roi.

The schedule suffered. The bombardment of both islands began on time, but the landing operation lost ground. Altogether, twenty-four 10th Amtrac Battalion LVTs couldn't even be located. The 23d Marines conquered its woes by 1100 hours, but the 24th didn't. Then some extra tractors were found, but there

Amtracs and landing craft laden with Marines bound for Roi wait offshore while errant amtracs are corralled and sent forward to fill gaps in the invasion-bound company formations. *Official USMC Photo*

These untested Marines still show signs of cockiness as they wait aboard a landing craft for an amtrac that will convey them the rest of the way to Roi and their sobering baptism in blood. *Official USMC Photo*

were not enough in total for both assault battalions of the 24th Marines—which finally lined up, each at two-thirds of its planned assault strength. And so forth; stuff just kept happening.

The 23d Marines was ready to go at 1100, but the order to land was withheld until 1112, to give the 24th Marines time to catch up. Despite a rain squall that threatened to break up last-minute air attacks, carrier bombers hovering beyond the maximum ordinate of artillery, ships' fire, and rockets were able to deliver pinpoint attacks down to almost the last minute before the first wave of amtracs ground onto both islands.

The Marines have landed. An infantry squad pauses on Roi's beach while, in the rear, an LVT(A) lands and drives forward to cover the inland advance. *Official USMC Photo*

ROI

Roi was almost harder to reach than it was to secure. Four companies of 1/23 and 2/23 landed abreast, with LVT(A)s in the vanguard. The LVT(A)s on the left hit the beach at 1133, and two companies of 1/23 were ashore by 1158. Resistance was negligible in the 1/23 zone, and the first phase line was taken in good order. Medium tanks and light flame tanks arrived ashore as 1/23 advanced on the airfield.

The action in the 2/23 zone was a little different. The LVT(A)s assigned to 2/23 stopped short to fire their 37mm guns at supposed defenses; then the troop-carrying amtracs ran past them to the beach. The infantry landed in some disarray due to alignment problems, but the Japanese were dazed by the heavy bombardment and nearly passive.

Roi was not defended in nearly the strength the planners had been led to believe. There were few formal defensive emplacements. Marine infantrymen were typically

continued on page 104

A 4th Tank Battalion Sherman moves up to engage a Japanese fighting position while Marine infantrymen take cover on the beach. Note the K-bar knife that has been embedded in a plank of wood in the center of this photo. *Official USMC Photo*

In a beachside aid station, navy hospital corpsmen work on a Marine who has suffered an injury to his right eye. *Official USMC Photo*

A pair of Marines armed with M1 rifles attempt to locate and neutralize a source of opposition that has sent them to ground during their unit's advance from the beach. *Official USMC Photo*

A platoon of medium tanks advances without infantry support. Overeager tank crews that did so throughout the day's fighting on Roi caused mounting dislocations in the carefully planned assault schedule when Marine infantrymen felt obligated to rush ahead to support them. *Official USMC Photo*

Most of Roi was given over to the airfield. This precluded an effective deep defense of the island, but it provided Japanese infantrymen and gunners holed up in bunkers, trenches, and pillboxes at the periphery of the airfield broad vistas for firing on the advancing 23d Marines. *Official USMC Photo*

This wire team is advancing across part of the airfield complex under close escort. It was essential to the conduct and coordination of a modern military effort that all combat units remain in close communication with higher headquarters. This was especially risky work in the wide, open spaces of Roi's airfield. *Official USMC Photo*

continued from page 101
cautious, but tanks and armored amtracs advanced without much support, some would say recklessly. This drew the infantry—dutiful in a pinch—northward in a running effort to provide support for the tanks. The headlong attack was a success even as it drove higher-level officers to distraction because they lost control of their organizations and their plans were rendered obsolete. It took until 1445 to get the tanks back under regimental control, and the infantry followed suit.

These are quibbles. The troops acted bravely and did what Marines are supposed to do if they see the opportunity, which is *seize* the opportunity.

A 37mm crew uses a wrecked Japanese bomber for cover as it sets in to support the assault on the airfield. In this instance, wide vistas aided the Marines. *Official USMC Photo*

This debris cloud marks the success of Marine assault engineers who have just blown up an active fighting position that had been holding up the advance across part of the airfield. *Official USMC Photo*

A wounded prisoner is treated by a corpsman as one Marine keeps his carbine poised and other Marines simply gawk. *Official USMC Photo*

At 1530, the lead battalions opened simultaneous, coordinated advances north along either shoreline. Aided by 75mm halftracks, 2/23 overcame organized resistance in its zone by 1600. On the left, 1/23 was a little slower getting started, but organized resistance in its zone collapsed by 1645. By 1800, the assault battalions were in complete control of Roi's entire shoreline, and 3/23 was at work prying a few defiant defenders from the interior as well as establishing a line to seal Roi from Namur by way of the sandspit that connected the islands.

continued on page 110

Ammunition in a pillbox that had apparently been detonated during the prelanding bombardment is still cooking off as the position is approached by Marines on February 1. *Official USMC Photo*

A pair of Marine officers discusses options for reaching across a broad, open expanse to the undoubtedly defended hangar and reinforced concrete building in the background. Tanks are still running wild and cannot be called on to help. *Official USMC Photo*

Riflemen cover the advance of Marine assault engineers who have been directed to blow up as much of the distant hangar and concrete building as they can. *Official USMC Photo*

Marines assigned to mop up this partially demolished building have discovered that it is a storehouse for aerial bombs, some of which are strewn in the open. *Official USMC Photo*

These Japanese corpses have been pulled into the open from a blown bunker, a precaution to make sure they're all dead as well as to make it easy to search for useful data they might be carrying. *Official USMC Photo*

Prisoners are put to work gathering corpses of their countrymen and dumping them into shell craters for burial. *Official USMC Photo*

Left and below: Roi was an easy victory for Marines who had been briefed on the terrible fighting at Tarawa, but it came at a cost. *Official USMC Photos*

continued from page 106

NAMUR

The 24th Marines had problems in spades with its quota of troop-carrying amtracs, but four assault companies were launched toward the beach in decent order. The plan was for LVT(A)s to land ahead of the troops and clear routes off the beaches. But the LVT(A)s ran afoul of antitank ditches, trenches, and debris; they could not advance as planned. Initially, they could only support the infantry by fire.

The leading infantry waves became misaligned as they neared the beach because landmarks that were supposed to guide the landing had either been pulverized by the bombardment or were invisible beneath a pall of smoke and dust. The two lead companies of 2/24, on the right beach, became intermingled, but the superbly trained troops formed into ad hoc assault teams where necessary and racked up some quick advances. The rest of 2/24 landed as amtracs became available, and these troops were fed into a gap that quickly developed in the battalion front line. The deepest penetration in the 2/24 zone was 175 yards, but resistance stiffened appreciably at that point, and the troops were pinned down in thick brush.

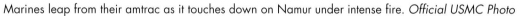

Marines leap from their amtrac as it touches down on Namur under intense fire. *Official USMC Photo*

Thick black smoke rises from a Japanese oil dump that has been set on fire by the naval bombardment. *Official USMC Photo*

A corpsman fills in a casualty evacuation tag for a Marine who has been wounded in the opening minutes of the assault on Namur. *Official USMC Photo*

Five carrier bombers pass right over the Namur beachhead on their way to bomb Japanese positions in the northern part of the island.
Official USMC Photo

On the regimental left, 3/24's two lead companies came ashore in better order than the adjacent 2/24 units, and they advanced quickly to the phase line halfway across Namur. The fighting on Namur was trickier than on Roi because Roi was mostly hard-topped runway and taxiways, while Namur was covered with thick growth in which the Japanese could easily hide and dig in. Hard-to-find emplacements were bypassed by the lead units, left to be reduced by the regimental reserve, 1/24.

Only three of five light tanks assigned to support 3/24 landed at 1300. Two bogged down in soft sand, and the third ran into a shell crater. All three were towed free after the two remaining light tanks landed.

One company of 3/24 advanced 150 yards beyond the phase line, but it withdrew when the battalion reorganized.

At 1305, a demolitions team in the 2/24 zone attacked a large concrete bunker with satchel charges and thus set off a huge uncharted torpedo dump. The immense blast leveled the bunker, set off two nearby ammunition dumps, and took down a good deal of the growth and other buildings around it. The multiple blasts killed twenty 2/24 Marines and injured more than a hundred.

Shocked, dazed, and further disorganized by the blast, 2/24 was unable to step off with 3/24 at 1630 for what the commanders hoped would be a final drive to secure the

continued on page 115

Marines of 2/24 sort themselves out after two companies were mislanded at the outset of the assault. Through the smoke-laden air, a U.S. Navy destroyer can be seen as it stands by close to shore to offer direct fire support. *Official USMC Photo*

Tanks are put ashore from LCTs and LCMs. For the first time, Marine tanks are equipped with fording kits that are able to supply air to their engines even if they have to run a few feet underwater. Many of the tanks that attempted to land at Betio were swamped in deep shell craters, and the fording kits were designed and fabricated in weeks. The Sherman in the center of the photo still has the entire kit aboard, but the light tank at the far right has shed the stack. The lower ductwork is bolted to the tank's air intake. *Official USMC Photo*

A wounded Marine is carried into a beachside aid station. *Official USMC Photo*

This medium tank has just caved in a log bunker overlooking the landing beaches. *Official USMC Photo*

A rifle squad that has paused beside a demolished beachside pillbox prepares to move inland. Note the Japanese machine gun that rests atop the pillbox. *Official USMC Photo*

island. But a herculean effort by the 2/24 officers and troops sent the battalion and an array of light and medium tanks back into the advance at 1730.

By late afternoon, elements of 2/24 had driven to within thirty-five yards of the northern shore. The battalion main body could not close on it, so this force was pulled back.

The division commander landed on Namur at 1700 and immediately asked the 24th Marines commander what he needed—which all came down to more troops. A platoon of medium tanks and 3/23 were transferred to the 24th Marines' control and ordered to cross from Roi via the sandspit.

The 3/24 battalion commander ordered the medium tanks to spearhead a new drive as soon as they reached his command post at 1830. This brought Marines to Namur's northwestern point, but low ammunition supplies obliged them to pull back to the 3/24 main body. At 1930, the regimental commander ordered all the troops on Namur to halt, consolidate, dig in, and prepare to make a final sweep at dawn. Fully two-thirds of Namur was solidly in Marine hands when the sun went down.

continued on page 128

Holed up for the moment under cover of a seawall, these Marines discuss options for breaking cover to begin the advance inland. *Official USMC Photo*

Below: This scene is unusual in that .50-caliber heavy machine guns were used almost exclusively as vehicle weapons or light antiaircraft guns, not as infantry weapons. This might be part of an experiment to test the half-inch bullets against fortified positions. Note that the gunner is still wearing his inflatable life belt, an accouterment most Marines dumped as early as possible. *Official USMC Photo*

As the advancing infantry spread inland, battalion and regimental communicators rushed to install and maintain a regimentwide communications network. *Official USMC Photo*

A light tank passes through an infantry command post on its way to help spark an advance at the front. *Official USMC Photo*

A Marine braves Japanese fire to advance through a blasted stand of trees. In the center of the thick smoke ahead is a burning Japanese block-house. *Official USMC Photo*

The Japanese on Namur put up a courageous defense on D-day, but they were overwhelmed wherever they fought. *Official USMC Photo*

The immense, shocking detonation of the uncharted torpedo dump at 1305 hours was captured on film by an aerial observer as the dense black smoke cloud enshrouds most of eastern Namur. *Official U.S. Navy Photo*

This page and opposite: Numerous buildings and defensive emplacements on Namur were built from steel-reinforced concrete that stood up well to all but the heaviest or most accurate fire. Even positions that had been penetrated during the prelanding bombardment provided formidable cover, and Japanese seeking cover in the rubble were difficult to pry out. When a concrete emplacement was blown up, shards of concrete took on the characteristics of shrapnel and could prove deadly to attackers as well as defenders. Typically, it took guts and patience to advance on a defensive emplacement, take it out, and then comb through the rubble. *Official USMC Photos*

Sometimes guts and skill weren't enough.
Official USMC Photos

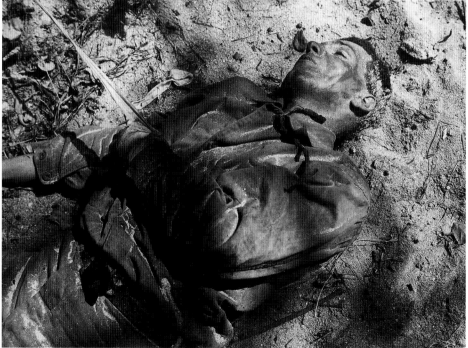

Now that Marines had fully embraced modern tank-infantry tactics, Marine M3s and M4s played a pivotal role in unlocking the Japanese defenses on Namur. *Official USMC Photo*

This Marine light tank, a company commander's vehicle, was assaulted on Namur by Japanese infantry when it became hung up after straying ahead of Marine lines. The Japanese killed two crewmen outright, wounded another, and mortally wounded the company commander before Marine infantry could organize a counterattack. Note that the hull above the track has been breached by an antitank round and that a Japanese soldier is pinned beneath the tank treads. *Official USMC Photo*

This light machine gun squad is staying close to the ground in a smoky, fireswept corner of Namur's twisted forest. *Official USMC Photo*

These Marines have found good cover in a Japanese-dug trench. They will use the cover as far as possible as they probe forward. *Official USMC Photo*

Marines who have dropped explosives into an underground hideaway wait for survivors to exit the smoke-filled chamber. A ghostlike figure appears to be standing in the center of the billowing black cloud. *Official USMC Photo*

A squad leader motions for his men to keep their heads well below the rim of the shell crater in which they have sought cover. *Official USMC Photo*

This Japanese light tank was probably damaged during the preinvasion bombardment. *Official USMC Photo*

This Marine infantry squad is preparing to go "over the top" and leapfrog ahead as far as it can in continuous short rushes. *Official USMC Photo*

Whenever possible, riflemen in the advance liked to be covered by light machine guns, like this one, or by BARS—anything that might give defenders an excuse to keep their heads down. *Official USMC Photo*

These Marines are probably dueling a small Japanese group that has gone to ground in another part of the rubble. The Marine at the far right has just hurled a hand grenade. *Official USMC Photo*

This infantry company command post has been set up on the fly in a relatively intact building far enough behind the front lines to allow the headquarters troops to relax a bit. The break for the night on Namur gave command groups like this one some time to account for and reorganize their assets, to report to and receive directions from higher headquarters, and to oversee resupply of subordinate units. *Official USMC Photo*

The Japanese pushed back into the last corner of Namur under their control and found a gap in Marine lines that they attempted to infiltrate—not to escape but to sow confusion and inflict casualties. Marines responded with overwhelming force. *Official USMC Photo*

continued from page 115

D+1

The Japanese mounted a few desultory attacks during the night, and a lot of Marines fired at spooky targets that were most likely imaginary. Ammunition was distributed to the troops, but the medium tanks could not access ammunition and fuel stored on Roi, so they pooled what they had, stripping one M4 tank in the process.

Also during the night, Japanese troops located a gap between Company I, 3/24, and Company B, 1/24. They infiltrated in force and launched a counterattack at first light. The four medium tanks and infantrymen on both sides of the gap held the attackers at bay, Marine reinforcements counterattacked, and the action ended in twenty-five minutes. Indeed, tanks and infantry used the opportunity to advance an extra fifty yards.

The attack in the 3/24 zone jumped off on schedule at 0900, and the battalion was in complete control of its objectives by 1215. The attack in the larger right zone was to be undertaken by 2/24 and most of 1/24. Tanks were late getting into position, so the attack jumped off late, at 1006. Light and medium tanks and 75mm halftracks took on a number of blockhouses, bunkers, and pillboxes, and the infantry attacked steadily in good order. Namur was completely in Marine hands by 1215, and the island was declared secure at 1418 hours, February 2, 1944. It took the 7th Infantry Division until February 4 to secure Kwajalein, its larger and better-defended objective.

A Japanese counterattack at first light on D+1 was demolished. *Official USMC Photo*

When tanks were late getting to the front lines to support the final Marine attack on Namur, 75mm halftracks spearheaded the assault. *Official USMC Photo*

The last defensive positions remaining in Japanese hands were smothered in heavy fire, leaving the defenders with a choice of dying by fire or dying by gunfire. *Official USMC Photo*

As soon as Namur was declared secure on February 2, 1944, many Marines were put to work scouring the island for bypassed Japanese. *Official USMC Photo*

Many of the last remaining defenders killed themselves rather than be taken alive. *Official USMC Photos*

Several Japanese were taken alive. One other survivor turned out to be a Marshall Islander, a woman. *Official USMC Photos*

Official USMC Photo

PLANNING ENIWETOK

Next up was a bold 350-mile jump to Eniwetok Atoll, at the western edge of the Marshall Islands. Eniwetok was one of only a few firm targets developed from a long list of potential bases drawn up before the Marshalls invasion. The seizure of Eniwetok had been penciled in for May, but several factors contributed to an immediate landing in the wake of the Kwajalein coup de main. These were the complete vindication of the tactics of the Kwajalein operation; the ease of the operation; the location of charts of Eniwetok that would otherwise have taken months to compile; and the availability of all the troops, equipment, and ships needed for an immediate invasion.

The fleet elements were drawn from portions of the Kwajalein invasion fleet, and ground troops were mainly the reinforced independent 22d Marines and two-thirds of the 27th Infantry Division's 106th Infantry Regiment, both of which had been the Kwajalein reserve; they were all well-trained troops, ready to go.

Planning was done on the fly based on remarkably accurate ad hoc intelligence estimates. As with the use of heavier naval firepower, the landing plan was able to incorporate valuable immediate lessons from Kwajalein.

Three of Eniwetok's four main islands were targeted for amphibious assaults: Engebi and Parry by Marines, and Eniwetok by the army troops. It was estimated that three thousand fresh Japanese troops held these islands, about a third of the total on each. Engebi was the site of a newly built airfield, never used by the Japanese; it was the atoll's primary strategic objective, followed by the anchorage.

The 22d Marines had served eighteen months of garrison duty in Samoa and thus was considered well trained and cohesive to the lowest organizational levels. Its organization was a hybrid first fielded by the 2d Raider Battalion in 1942: infantry squads were divided into three four-man or four three-man fire teams. This meant that the regiment fielded an extra level of command at its lowest level—corporals and privates first class with hands-on authority that would offset the natural balkanization of infantry units on the modern battlefield.

An aerial view of Engebi, looking north to south. *Official USMC Photo*

ENGEBI

As at Kwajalein, the decision was made to land first on several tiny islands from which Engebi—the first target—could be interdicted by artillery fire. Thus, on February 17, 1944, the V Amphibious Corps Reconnaissance Company went ashore on five of these islands, and the 2d Separate Pack Howitzer Battalion and an army 105mm howitzer battalion were emplaced on two of the islands by nightfall. Also on February 17, navy underwater demolition teams (UDTs) made their combat debut to examine the beaches off Engebi, and that night the 4th Marine Division reconnaissance company (Company D, 4th Tank Battalion) landed by rubber boat on two more small islands off Engebi to seal the Japanese on Engebi to that island.

As three assault waves of Marines approach Engebi's southwestern coast in army amtracs, the final prelanding bombardment strikes the island. Note the immense number of shell craters throughout Engebi. *Official U.S. Navy*

Below: The Engebi beachhead viewed from a second-wave amtrac. *Official USMC Photo*

Members of the 22d Marines move inland to dig out a sniper. *Official USMC Photo*

A hospital corpsman must keep his head low as he treats a wounded Marine on the beach. Japanese fire is passing low overhead. *Official USMC Photo*

These Marines were killed as they advanced inland. *Official USMC Photo*

Following a massive artillery, naval gunfire, and air bombardment down to only minutes before the landing, 1/22 and 2/22 landed abreast on the southwestern side of triangular Engebi shortly after 0800 on February 19. The movement to the beaches was so smooth that the final air attacks had to be truncated. Carrying the first wave was an army amtrac battalion that included a full company of LVT(A)s (which the soldiers called amtanks). There were several minor dislocations, but the amtrac crewmen, who had landed at Kwajalein Island, knew what they were about, and organizational mixing was kept to a minimum.

Much of the ground was heavily wooded and quite tangled, but the Marine infantry seized a lodgment and relentlessly worked outward from it. Marine tanks landed in good order, just in time to help the infantry take out Japanese tanks dug in as pillboxes. By 1030 hours, 2/22, on the left, had seized the airfield and all its other objectives except the island's western and northern points.

On the right, 1/22 ran into tangled underbrush that was more heavily defended than the hard-topped airfield. Progress was slower and less cohesive. When a gap in the battalion front developed, a company of 3/22 advanced to fill it. The fighting here was especially difficult, but in the meantime one of 1/22's companies, aided by a pair of army 105mm self-propelled assault guns, overcame the defensive key point in the battalion zone, a cluster of concrete pillboxes on the southern point.

As the heavy fighting in the 1/22 zone gobbled up the regimental reserves, 2/22 took the last defensive positions on its part of the island by 1322 hours. The ground commander declared the island secure at 1450 hours, and six minutes later 1/22 overcame the last defensive sector in its zone. Almost immediately, 3/22 and the 2d Separate Tank Company were ordered to reembark to serve as the reserve for landings the next day on Eniwetok Island by army troops.

continued on page 142

As the main bodies of 1/22 and 2/22 advance inland, patrols work the beachhead to clear out bypassed Japanese fighting positions. *Official USMC Photos*

Above: A squad leader at far left admonishes his men to spread out as they advance across flat, open ground. *Official USMC Photo*

Left: A Marine passes a dead Japanese soldier as he hustles toward cover ahead. *Official USMC Photo*

Sherman tanks of the 2d Separate Tank Company, supporting 2/22, can be seen at the bottom of this panoramic view—taken by a carrier fighter pilot during a rocket attack—as they sweep around the northeastern end of the airfield. *Official U.S. Navy*

A close-up of the same scene, taken moments later. *Official U.S. Navy Photo*

Mopping up. *Official USMC Photo*

Official USMC Photo

Following a bloodless landing and orderly move to its zone of action during the afternoon of February 19, a 3/22 medium machine gun engages a Japanese beachside machine gun nest about four hundred yards to the west. *Official USMC Photo*

ENIWETOK ISLAND

Early during the assault against Eniwetok Island, the army commander realized that he could not easily take the island with only two infantry battalions. Therefore, 3/22 was sent ashore midway through D-day, February 19, and assigned to sweep half of the southwestern third of the island beside one of the army battalions. An afternoon attack meant to secure the southwestern part of the island went awry because, depending on who tells it, the army battalion lagged or the Marine battalion advanced too quickly. Both units advanced after sunset with the aid of artillery illumination, and they lost contact again as they moved ahead at different rates. The Marines reached the tip of the island, assured by their army counterparts that the battalions were in contact in the center. This proved to be wrong; the Japanese infiltrated the long breach and counterattacked at dawn. Nonetheless, following several heart-stopping assaults by the cornered Japanese, the Americans prevailed. It took almost all of February 20 to scour southwestern Eniwetok, and it took yet another day for the second army battalion to secure the northeastern half of the island.

continued on page 148

Pages 143–145: As soon as it reached its sector in Eniwetok's southwestern quadrant, 3/22 mounted a rapid advance that overwhelmed all opposition and outpaced the army infantry battalion operating on its right flank. *Official USMC Photos*

This page and opposite: After beating back a Japanese counterattack at dawn, 3/22 resumed its rapid advance and—not without paying a price—secured its sector of Eniwetok late in the afternoon on February 20. *Official USMC Photos*

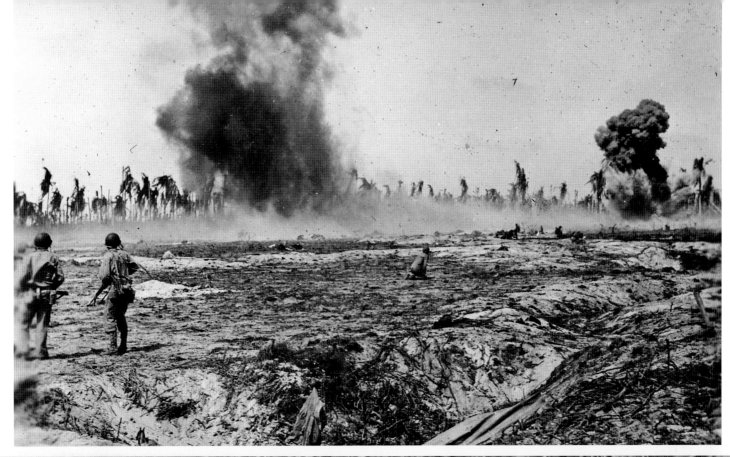

A number of Marines were killed by mines as they came ashore on Parry. *Official USMC Photo*

PARRY

Taking Parry Island turned out to be quite messy. The army amtracs were facing their fourth amphibious assault since February 1, and it showed; a lot of the equipment was worn or even sidelined, and the crewmen were physically and emotionally exhausted. The 22d Marines was having problems, too. Its battalions had suffered losses on Engebi and Eniwetok that could not be replaced, only rejiggered, and there were even looming ammunition shortages that had to be factored into the Parry plan. The troops also needed M1 rifles and BARs that many had replaced ahead of the battles with lighter carbines that simply did not have the offensive lethality they learned they needed.

Despite ammunition rationing, the Parry landings, on February 22, pulled down almost too much artillery and naval gunfire support. The invasion beaches on the northwestern coast were so obscured by dust and smoke that many elements of 1/22 and 2/22 didn't know they had been mislanded and intermingled until well into the action—so much so that gunfire support was mistakenly called on top of friendlies who believed they were someplace else.

continued on page 154

Left and below: If it's possible, there was *too much* naval gunfire support as the 22d Marines went ashore on Parry. The smoke and dust were so thick that elements of the two assault battalions were landed by disoriented amtrac drivers as many as three hundred yards off their mark and badly intermingled. Then, as the battalions both sorted themselves out and opened their advance from the beach, naval gunfire guided through the smoke by radar began to fall on the troops they were meant to support. *Official USMC Photos*

This page: Inland lay thick, tangled growth infested by hundreds of Japanese in both prepared and improvised fighting positions. About the only way to spot such positions was by drawing fire. *Official USMC Photos*

Parry was small, so even 60mm mortars did not have to displace as much as normal to keep pace with the riflemen. The empty ammunition canisters that litter this mortar position attest to a busy day. *Official USMC Photo*

Four wounded Marines arrive beside a navy transport aboard an army DUKW in time to have their photo taken by a coast guard photographer. *Official Coast Guard Photo*

This page: The 2d Separate Tank Company's Shermans provided the 22d Marines with an essential boost during the fighting on Parry. One tank was temporarily sidelined when it bogged down on the beach, but the remainder were in the thick of the fighting throughout the day even though the crews had weathered a wringing twenty-five-mile overnight trip from Engebi aboard LCTs. *Official USMC Photos*

Lightly armored with no overhead cover, the 22d Marines' 75mm half-tracks also provided yeoman service on Parry as stand-off weapons that could destroy or at least buffet pillboxes the infantrymen located in the thickets. *Official USMC Photo*

Above and left: A dawn attack on February 23 overcame Parry's last pocket of resistance by 0900 hours. *Official USMC Photos*

continued from page 148

Tangled undergrowth and trees, not to mention Japanese troops motivated to fight unto death, made Parry a hell on earth throughout D-day. The plan for postlanding operations was complicated, especially for troops and troop leaders who were emotionally wrung out. After 2/22 had crossed the island, it was to go into regimental reserve. The initial reserve, 3/22, was then to go into the attack down the long north-south axis of the island to the right of 1/22, which had come ashore on 2/22's right and which was to wheel 90 degrees and dress on 3/22's line. This is a complicated maneuver for fresh troops.

The left battalion, 2/22, took all its objectives by 1400, and 1/22 managed to secure a lot of ground despite heavy casualties. The Japanese bungled their best chance to halt the American advance by withholding their three tanks until American tanks had reached the 1/22 front. A Japanese counterattack employing all three tanks was bloodily repulsed. Remarkably, falling into the vacuum created by the immolation of the Japanese main force, 1/22 secured its entire zone, flawlessly completed the requisite 90-degree pivot, and stood ready to advance down Parry's long axis beside 3/22 at 1330 hours.

Medium tanks made all the difference, as they had wherever they had been landed so far in the Pacific. By sunset, the regimental front stood 450 yards from Parry's southern tip, which is to say that Marines had secured more than two thousand yards during the day. The attack was halted at sunset to avoid accidental intramural fighting in the dark, and even though Japanese troops were still out ahead, the island was declared secure.

Snipers engaged the Marines during the night, but casualties were light. The offensive resumed at dawn on February 23, the last defenses were overwhelmed by 0900, and one of the army battalions, held in reserve, turned to scouring the island for stragglers. The 10th Defense Battalion, which had stood up five ad hoc infantry companies as a force reserve for Parry, remained behind, as did the army battalions, when the exhausted 22d Marines sailed from Eniwetok on February 25.

With two or three assault landings under his belt in only a week's time, this young Marine savors a cup of hot coffee and must be thinking about a shower and sleep, not necessarily in that order. *Official USMC Photo*

Many Japanese-occupied atolls and islands in the Marshalls were to be bypassed and contained by aerial interdiction alone, but the status of many individual islands had to be determined by Marines and soldiers on the ground. Shown here, an army amtrac covers Marines from the VAC Reconnaissance Company as they sweep across an island that proves to be unoccupied. *Official USMC Photo*

TAKING STOCK

The Marshalls campaign, which engulfed yet more atolls over several months, painted two bold strokes across the first Japanese mandate to fall into Allied hands. As far as the American commanders were concerned, U.S. forces had breached the outer skin of the Empire of Japan and, as such, stood on line to breach a few vital organs.

The March 30 landing by Marines on this island was briefly opposed by a handful of Japanese. One Marine was killed here, two Marines were wounded, and all the Japanese died. *Official USMC Photo*

This page and the following: The airfields on Roi (seen here) and Eniwetok were rapidly repaired and expanded to serve as way stations on the main central Pacific air route, and hosted 4th Marine Air Wing combat squadrons that guarded the bases and anchorages against aerial hecklers, provided antisubmarine patrols, and mounted almost continuous attacks against bypassed Japanese bases. Other airfields, especially the big one on Kwajalein, hosted large Army Air Forces bombers and full-service field hospitals served by air evacuation flights. *Official USMC Photos*

Bibliography

Books

Blakeney, Jane. *Heroes: U.S. Marine Corps, 1861–1955.* Washington, D.C.: Blakeney Publishing, 1956.

Hammel, Eric. *Air War Pacific: Chronology, America's Air War Against Japan in East Asia and the Pacific, 1941–1945.* Pacifica, Calif.: Pacifica Press, 1998.

———. *Pacific Warriors: The U.S. Marines in World War II, A Pictorial Tribute.* St. Paul: Zenith Press, 2005.

Hammel, Eric, and John E. Lane. *Bloody Tarawa.* St. Paul: Zenith Press, 2006.

Shaw, Henry I. Jr., Bernard C. Nalty, and Edwin T. Turnbladh. *Central Pacific Drive: History of U.S. Marine Corps Operations in World War II,* Vol. III. Washington, D.C.: United States Marine Corps, 1966.

Toland, John. *The Rising Sun: The Decline and Fall of the Japanese Empire, 1936–1945.* New York: Random House, 1970.

Williams, Mary H. *Chronology, 1941–1945: United States Army in World War II.* Washington, D.C.: Office of the Chief of Military History, 1960.

Periodical
Hammel, Eric. "The Invasion of Tarawa." *Leatherneck Magazine*, November 1984.

Index